An American Bird Conservancy Compact Guide

Paul Lehman
Ornithological Editor

American Bird Conservancy (ABC) is a U.S.-based, not-for-profit organization whose mission is to conserve wild birds and their habitats throughout the Americas. It is the only U.S.-based group dedicated solely to addressing the greatest threats facing birds in the Western Hemisphere. A growing human population is critically impacting bird populations through habitat destruction, direct mortality from such harmful practices as the unwise use of pesticides, and the introduction of invasive species, including free-roaming domestic animals. ABC believes adequate resources exist to overcome these threats and that unifying people, organizations, and agencies around common approaches to priority issues is the key to success.

ABC draws on people and organizations through bird conservation networks—including the North American Bird Conservation Initiative, Partners in Flight, the ABC Policy Council, and ABC's growing international network—to address the most critical issues affecting birds. It builds partnerships of conservation groups, scientists, and the public to tackle these conservation priorities, one by one, using the best skills and expertise available. The key to ABC's unique approach lies in supporting and facilitating these networks without controlling them, establishing consensus on priorities using the best science available, developing collaborative solutions, and then openly sharing credit for successes with its partners. ABC measures its success in terms of changes on the ground for the benefit of target species, populations, and habitats.

ABC members receive *Bird Conservation*, the magazine providing in-depth coverage of American bird conservation by all agencies and groups, and *Bird Calls*, the newsletter covering the full range of bird conservation issues and activities.

For more information, please see these websites:

ABC and the ABC Council: *www.abcbirds.org*
North American Bird Conservation Initiative:
www.nabci.org
North American Waterbird Conservation Plan:
www.nacwcp.org
North American Waterfowl Management Plan:
www.nawmp.ca
Partners in Flight: *www.partnersinflight.org*
United States Shorebird Conservation Plan:
www.manomet.org/USSCP/index.htm

ALL THE
BACKYARD
BIRDS
W E S T

BY JACK L. GRIGGS

Red-shafted Flicker

HarperResource
An Imprint of HarperCollins*Publishers*

Dedicated to V. Frances Griggs

Designed by Jack L. Griggs & Peg Alrich
Edited by Virginia Croft
Illustrations reformatted by Jack E. Griggs
from the original illustrations published in
All the Birds of North America
by the following artists:

F. P. Bennett p. 29; John Dawson pp. 41–51,
73, 75; Dale Dyer pp. 77–89; Larry McQueen pp. 63–71;
Hans Peeters pp. 19–25, 31, 33, 53–61; Doug Pratt pp. 35–39;
and Andrew Vallely p. 27.

HarperCollins books may be purchased for educational, business, or sales promotional use. For information please write: Special Markets Department, HarperCollins Publishers Inc., 10 East 53rd Street, New York, NY 10022.

First HarperResource paperback edition published 2003

Library of Congress Cataloging-in-Publication Data has been applied for.
ISBN 0-06-053336-6 (pbk.)
03 04 05 06 PE 10 9 8 7 6 5 4 3 2 1

CONTENTS

HOW TO ATTRACT BIRDS
a foreword by Scott Edwards 6

HOW TO ATTRACT BIRDS

by
SCOTT EDWARDS

There are four fundamental attractions for birds: food, water, shelter, and a place to raise their young, all of which are easily provided in backyards.

Food is the most basic and obvious bird attraction, and more birds are attracted to black-oil sunflower seeds ("oilers" to bird-feeding veterans) than to any other seed. The black-oil sunflower seeds are smaller compared to the more familiar large striped varieties. Other attractive seeds are thistle seeds, striped sunflower seeds, split peanuts, peanuts in the shell, white proso millet, and various nuts.

It is important to note that not everything labeled "birdseed" is eaten by birds. Many birdseed mixes contain filler products, seeds that add only weight and actually detract from the mix's attractiveness. Grains like milo, oats, wheat, rice, and canary seed, as well as the ambiguous "mixed grain products," are best avoided. Table scraps are not recommended for birds either. Bread crumbs, crackers, and similar foods are just empty calories that offer very little nutrition.

When most people think of bird feeding, they think first of offering seed. However, only a

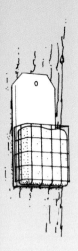

minority of the birds that surround us are seed-crushers. Many additional birds can be attracted to your feeding station if you offer suet, fruit, mealworms, or nectar.

Suet is the fat that surrounds beef kidneys. It will attract woodpeckers, chickadees, titmice, nuthatches, and brown creepers. It is also occasionally eaten by catbirds, mockingbirds, orioles, and warblers, among others. Suet is very dense and should not be confused with fat trimmings from other beef parts. Plain fat is not as beneficial, has a much higher water content, and will freeze in cold weather.

Suet is not just for winter feeding. Most commercially available suets have been rendered, meaning that they have been boiled repeatedly to remove impurities and to prevent them from going rancid. There is even "summer suet" or suet doughs that are made to survive hot weather without melting.

Suet is best attached directly to the trunk of a large deciduous tree, at least initially. This is where the birds that feed on suet look for their food in the wild.

Fruit like oranges, grapes, and bananas attract orioles and tanagers. Bug-eating birds such

as bluebirds, wrens, and many others readily take mealworms. And, of course, no feeding station would be complete without the presence of nectar for hummingbirds.

The accepted formula for hummingbird nectar is four to five parts water to one part plain table sugar. I don't recommend the use of commercially prepared nectars or the use of coloring. Do not use any artificial sweeteners or honey. It is important to maintain a nectar feeder regularly. Nectar ferments rapidly and can be hazardous to hummingbirds if left out for more than a day or two. Nectar should be changed more often in hot weather.

How to dispense bird food, particularly seed, is an important choice to make. There are three basic designs for seed feeders: the tube feeder, usually made of polycarbonate and designed to hang from a tree or hook; the open platform feeder, which may or may not be covered; and the hopper feeder, basically a platform feeder with a Plexiglas center (the hopper) to hold and dispense seed.

Most tube feeders are designed to dispense black-oil sunflower seeds. Nearly all of the small seed-eaters that perch on tube feeders have such a strong preference for oilers that

8

using a mixture of seeds is often counter-productive. If you are presently filling your tube feeders with mixed seeds, you probably have witnessed the birds employing a technique called "bill sweeping." By sweeping their beaks from side to side, the birds remove everything but the oilers. And you get to fill your tubes more often.

Some tube feeders have very small ports designed to dispense thistle (technically known as niger) seed. These feeders primarily attract goldfinches.

All tube feeders are designed for small birds. The jays, cardinals, grosbeaks, grackles, and woodpeckers are too big to use them. This is good for the small seed-eaters, which are often bullied off feeders that will accommodate larger birds. But if you can only have one feeder, you should consider a hopper feeder.

Hopper feeders are the most popular type, and a well-designed one will provide enough room to attract a large variety of birds. Both perching birds and ground feeders will visit a hopper feeder with a large landing area. The large seed capacity of the hopper feeder is another attractive feature for the people who have to fill them. Many hopper feeders will hold several pounds of birdseed and don't have to be filled every day. Because of the variety of birds a hopper feeder can attract, it is an excellent place to use a high-quality mixture of seeds.

The platform or fly-through feeder attracts perhaps the widest variety of birds. The open design of these feeders allows birds to come and go from all directions. There is no dispensing mechanism to clog, so you are free to use virtually any food or combination of foods. Use peanuts in the shell if you want regular visits from jays, nutcrackers, and woodpeckers. These feeders are also ideal for serving fruit during the warmer months. I attach suet to my platform feeder to increase visits from woodpeckers, titmice, chickadees, and nuthatches.

About four times a year it is a good idea to give your feeders a thorough cleaning. Feeders can get dirty, and wet seed can mold rapidly, making a feeding station unhealthy. Once a season I take down all my feeders over the course of a few days, hose them, soak them in a strong solution of white vinegar, and scrub them with a long-handled brush designed for feeder cleaning. I use vinegar, not bleach, because of the toxicity of chlorine and the fact that it can cloud tube feeders. Regular cleaning will help ensure a healthy feeding station in your yard.

All birds must drink and bathe, so the inclusion of a birdbath with a dripper or mister will greatly enhance the attractiveness of your backyard habitat to birds, as can a recirculating pond. Drippers and misters are accessories that attach to your outside water source and provide fresh, moving water for birds. Most drippers utilize a low-flow system that constantly drips water into your water feature.

Misters spray the area around your water feature with a fine mist. They are especially effective if your water feature is surrounded by foliage. While some birds hesitate to immerse themselves, they may "leaf-bathe," an action that has them rubbing their feathers against wet leaves. Misters are also very attractive to hummingbirds, which love to fly around in the mist these accessories create.

Nest boxes are used by many birds that nest in cavities (tree hollows). Bluebirds, nuthatches, wrens, and woodpeckers are a few of the species that will accept your hospitality if you erect the appropriate nest box. Some lucky people are even able to attract screech-owls!

Nest boxes should be made of untreated, unpainted wood. Red cedar or white pine 3/4 to 1 inch thick is preferable. Preservative, paints, or stains are unnecessary and may actually be harmful. The exact dimensions of the box vary depending on which bird you are attempting to attract. This information is readily available at any good library or nature center. Nest boxes must be maintained regularly and cleaned of nesting debris after each brood fledges. Keep a logbook on the progress of the birds using your nest boxes, especially one with bluebirds in it. All nest inspections should stop approximately ten days after the eggs hatch, or the nestlings may fledge prematurely.

Habitat enhancement is really the key to attracting the most interesting birds to your backyard. Successfully attracting a wide variety and number of birds to your backyard entails more than just supplying feeders, seed, a pond, or nest boxes, however. I have dozens of different feeders at my station, but there is more bird activity per square foot in my two brush piles (conglomerations of limbs, branches, and old Christmas trees) than anywhere else in my yard.

Juncos, towhees, and native sparrows such as the white-crowned nest and feed in the brush piles, and all the little songbirds seek cover there when a Cooper's or sharp-shinned hawk comes looking for an easy meal. If a brush pile is impractical, consider letting a small section of

your backyard go wild. Don't mow, don't prune, just let it grow and watch the birds show up!

Add fruit-bearing trees to your backyard habitat (mountain ash, hackberry, mulberry, and sassafras, for example) and you can attract waxwings, mockingbirds, warblers, and bluebirds. Coniferous trees and shrubs such as juniper and holly are wonderful bird attractions and provide cover as well as food.

You can find assistance in improving the attractiveness of your backyard habitat at your local nature center and at some of the better wild bird supply stores. Don't be discouraged if your first improvements don't get immediate results. Over time your backyard can become an oasis for birds.

Keep a good pair of binoculars on your windowsill next to this guide to identify the rarer birds your feeder attracts. Binoculars for birding should be 7 or 8 power, bright, sharp, and easy to hold. Stay away from cute gadgets like zooms, perma- or insta-focus, and strange-colored lenses. If you wear eyeglasses, you should be able to leave them on while using your binoculars. The wider your binoculars' field of vision (a salesperson can explain how this is measured), the easier they will be to use.

13

HOW TO LOOK AT A BIRD

The way birds feed and their adaptations for feeding are the most important points to recognize in identifying and understanding a bird. For the beginner, the color and pattern of an unknown bird can be so striking that important points of shape and behavior go unnoticed. But feeding adaptations, especially bill shape, best reveal a bird's role in nature — its truest identity.

Owls, hawks, doves, woodpeckers, and many other birds are easily recognized by shape and behavior. Songbirds are more confusing. If you don't immediately recognize a songbird as a sparrow, a wren, or a warbler, for example, look at its bill shape. Is it a seed-crusher or a bug-eater? Seed-crushers have strong, conical bills for cracking seeds. The shape of a bug-eater's bill varies with the way it catches bugs.

conical bill

Most bug-eaters have slender, straight bills used to probe in trees, brush, ground litter, and rock crevices. A few have curved bills for specialized probing. And some, the flycatcher group, have broad-based, flat bills. Flycatchers catch bugs in midair, and their broad bills improve their chances of success.

straight bill

curved bill

If bill shape can't be seen, a bird's feeding behavior is often just as revealing. Sparrows

flycatching bill

don't flit among the branches of a tree searching for bugs, and warblers won't be seen on the ground picking at seeds.

Knowing its bill shape or feeding behavior reduces the possible identities of an unknown bird. Plumage marks can then be used to identify all the backyard species.

Most names used to describe parts of a bird are predictable — back, crown, throat, etc. Three names that might not be immediately understood are rump, undertail coverts, and wing bars. The rump is at the base of the tail, topside; undertail coverts cover the base of the tail, bottomside. Wing bars are formed by the contrasting tips (often white) of the feathers that help cover the wing when it is folded.

Underside of tail showing tail spots and undertail coverts.

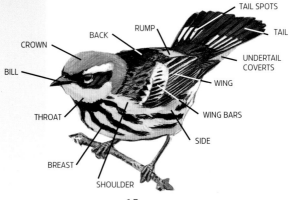

TAIL SPOTS

TAIL

RUMP

BACK

CROWN

UNDERTAIL COVERTS

BILL

WING

THROAT

WING BARS

SIDE

BREAST

SHOULDER

HOW TO READ THE MAPS

ange maps provide a simplified picture of a species' distribution. They indicate the birds that can be expected in any local region. Birds are not evenly distributed over their ranges. They require suitable habitat (no seeds, no sparrows) and are typically scarcest at their range limits. Some birds are numerous but not commonly seen because they are secretive.

Weather and food availability affect bird distribution in winter. Some birds regularly retreat south to escape winter weather. Others leave their northern ranges only occasionally. Some whose resident population slowly creeps northward in mild winters may perish if their newly occupied range is hit by a hard winter.

MAP KEY

SUMMER OR NESTING

WINTER

ALL YEAR

MIGRATION
(spring & fall)

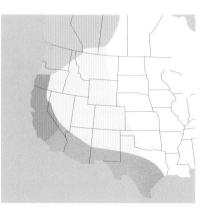

HOW THE BIRDS ARE ORGA- NIZED

OWLS AND NIGHTHAWK

GREAT HORNED OWL

BARN OWL

COMMON NIGHTHAWK

The western screech-owl has yellow eyes and distinctive horns but is only about the size of a man's hand. It visits woodsy parks and neighborhoods.

ecause they hunt in the evenings and at night, owls are not often seen in backyards — or anywhere else. But some of the more common owls live close to civilization and are likely to be heard. The great horned owl has proved particularly adaptable. It is the 800-pound gorilla of the bird world and goes almost anywhere it wants to, including parks and suburbs. It is large enough to take rabbits and ducks.

The **great horned owl** gives a series of distinctive low hoots in various rhythms: *hoo, hoo-hoo, hoo, hoo* or *hoo-hoo-hoo, hoo-hoo, hoo,* for instance. It is a massive bird with yellow eyes and large ear tufts, or "horns," which are usually raised and obvious.

Barn owls don't hoot but give a screech or rasping hiss. The white heart-shaped face set with dark eyes is its best visual mark. Barn owls hunt over fields and agricultural land. They fly close to the ground and are too often seen as road kill as a result of collisions with cars.

Nighthawks sweep through the sky feeding like swifts or swallows. They are common over open country and some towns and cities at dusk and dawn — sometimes in daylight. Note the **nighthawk's** white wing patch and listen for its nasal *peent* flight call.

18

Common
Nighthawk

Great Horned
Owl

Barn Owl

VULTURE AND CONDOR

TURKEY VULTURE

In southwestern deserts, the zone-tailed hawk mimics the flight and appearance of the turkey vulture in order to closely approach ground prey. White tail bands and a feathered head are its best distinguishing marks.

Large black birds with unfeathered heads tugging at a piece of road kill are easily recognized as vultures – the "buzzards" of the old West. And since there is only one vulture throughout most of the West, the **turkey vulture,** identification is not a problem. Adults are the ones with red heads. Young turkey vultures are dark-headed.

When not feeding, vultures are usually seen soaring high overhead in search of carrion. Even at a great distance, they can often be recognized by their flight style and the contrasting pattern of pale and dark on their underwing. Turkey vultures often tip a bit from side to side as they soar and usually hold their wings above horizontal in a shallow V.

Certainly not a common bird, the California condor is being nurtured back from near extinction. It has been reintroduced in Los Padres National Forest of California, and recently young birds have been released at the Grand Canyon, where they are more likely to be seen.

Young **California condors** (releases are all young birds) have dark heads. Their greater size and underwing pattern distinguish condors from vultures even at a distance.

20

young

Turkey Vulture

California Condor

HAWKS

KESTREL

RED-TAILED HAWK

The white-tailed kite is a hawk of open lands that has adapted to grassy highway borders in California, where it scans for rodents from a perch or hover.

The white-tailed kite is pale gray above with black shoulders, and white below with black wrist patches.

The kestrel and red-tailed hawk are not likely to be seen in backyards, but they are common along roads and in parks. A kestrel hunts from a perch, typically a wire or pole overlooking a vacant lot or other open area. It will often return to the same perch daily if it is successful in capturing the mice, large insects, or small birds that are its prey. Kestrels often hover over suspected prey.

The **kestrel** is identified by its small size, only 10 to 12 inches long, and two black face streaks contrasting with its white cheeks and throat. Males are smaller than females, and the blue on the male's wings contrasts sharply with the red on its back and tail. The female is an even red above, with heavy dark barring.

Red-tailed hawks are likely to be seen soaring overhead or perched on a roadside pole. Plumage varies considerably, but nearly all adults have a distinctive red tail (pink from below), with or without narrow dark tail bands. Young birds have brownish tails with many narrow dark bands. The dark streaking that often forms a band across a red-tail's belly is a good mark for many birds. And the dark bar along the leading edge of the underwing is a sure mark for identifying soaring birds.

pale
form

Kestrel
♀

♂

dark
form

intermediate
form

♂

pale
form

Red-tailed Hawk

intermediate
form

young

young

HAWKS

COOPER'S HAWK

SHARP-SHINNED HAWK

Young hawks of some larger species (buteos) can be confused with a young Cooper's, but they don't attack at backyard feeders as a Cooper's does. And a Cooper's seldom sits openly on roadside perches, as buteos do.

Cooper's and sharp-shinned hawks are the birds of prey known for attacking songbirds at backyard bird feeders and sometimes colliding with picture windows. They seldom perch openly like the hawks described on the previous page. Instead, they typically lurk in foliage until prey appears and then, with a sprinter's explosive burst, ambush the unsuspecting dinner.

Except in size, the two species are nearly identical. Both **Cooper's** and the **sharp-shinned** have long tails with distinctive broad dark and pale bands. Adults are blue-gray above with rusty barring below. Young birds are brown above and have brown streaking on their underparts.

Size differences between Cooper's and the sharp-shinned can be hard to judge. A small male sharpie (about 12 inches long) can be distinguished from a large female Cooper's (about 18 inches), but most individuals are somewhere in between. Small differences in their tails are the best marks separating the two species but are very difficult to see. The tip of a Cooper's tail is round and banded white. The sharpie's tail has squarer corners and a narrow gray terminal band.

Typical variations in
sharp-shinned hawk's tail

sharp-shinned
young

Cooper's

young

Cooper's young

sharp-shinned

young

adults shown in typical
flight; young birds soaring

Cooper's Hawk

young

**Sharp-shinned
Hawk**

young

SWALLOWS

CLIFF SWALLOW

TREE SWALLOW

BARN SWALLOW

Two other species are brown above and white below like young tree swallows. The bank swallow has a brown breast band; the rough-winged, a dirty-brown throat and upper breast.

Swallows are sleek and speedy aerialists that spend most of their day capturing bugs in flight. Because flying insects abound near water, swallows often fly over water. When not feeding, they can often be seen together, side by side on a wire by the dozens. Tree swallows commonly nest in boxes. Barn and cliff swallows make mud nests, often under eaves and bridges. The barn swallow's nest is cup shaped; the cliff swallow's, gourd shaped.

It isn't easy to get a good look at a flying swallow, but most species can be identified at a glance if you know what to look for. The **tree swallow** is white below and glossy blue-green above. (White on the similar violet-green swallow extends high onto the rump.) Young birds are brown above. Note that the tree swallow doesn't have a "swallowtail."

The **barn swallow** is the swallow with the tail shape that has become a graphic symbol of speed and grace. The upperparts are a deep blue on all birds, but the orange-buff under-parts can be paler on young birds. Young birds can also have shorter tail streamers.

The **cliff swallow** has a nearly square tail. Its buff rump contrasts with the dark back, and its dark throat contrasts with the pale breast and belly.

26

young

young

Cliff Swallow

Tree Swallow

Barn Swallow

HUMMING-BIRDS

RUFOUS
HUMMINGBIRD

ANNA'S
HUMMINGBIRD

BLACK-CHINNED
HUMMINGBIRD

BROAD-TAILED
HUMMINGBIRD

The jewel-like reflections from the throats (gorgets) of male hummers are only visible at favorable angles; most often the gorget appears dark. Watch for a flash of the gorget color as a hummer turns its head. Female hummers lack the male's distinctive gorget and can be very difficult to separate.

The rusty-colored back and sides of the male **rufous hummingbird** are an easy mark. Females have green backs. Along the coast of California, Allen's hummingbird is similar, but the adult male has a green back.

Anna's hummingbird is the most common hummer in West Coast backyards. The male has a rose-red crown and a flared gorget. The female is a bulky-looking version of the female black-chinned, with dingier-colored sides. Anna's is a bit larger than most hummers.

It is the band of purple on the male **black-chinned hummingbird's** gorget that is the important mark. Females are whitish below with a buff tinge on the sides.

Throughout much of the Rocky Mountains, the **broad-tailed hummingbird** is a regular at feeders. The male has a rose-red gorget; females look like female rufous hummers but are larger, with fuller tails and paler sides.

28

Rufous Hummingbird

♂

♀ rufous

Anna's
Hummingbird

♂

♀ black chinned

♂

Broad-tailed Hummingbird

Black-chinned
Hummingbird

♂

GAMEBIRDS

GAMBEL'S QUAIL

RING-NECKED PHEASANT

California quail can be separated from Gambel's by their call. The California gives a loud *chi-ca-go*; Gambel's adds a syllable, *chi-ca-go-go*.

Gamebirds have learned to be very cautious and to stay hidden for good reason. They are prey to many wild animals, as well as humans. Only a few gamebirds are found on cultivated land or in areas near people.

Quail venture into rural towns and backyards. They live and forage together in coveys (small flocks) most of the time. When nesting and raising young, they are paired. At night, they roost in trees for safety. The California quail is widespread; Gambel's is associated with desert scrub.

These are the only quail with teardrop-shaped plumes on their heads. The best marks separating them are on their bellies. The **California quail** has a scaled belly. The belly of **Gambel's quail** varies with sex. Males have a large black spot on their buff bellies that is lacking in females.

Ring-necked pheasants were introduced from Asia and are one of the few introduced gamebirds to become established. Some males have green bodies; others have white wings; some lack the neck ring. All males have a red eye patch. The most common form is illustrated. Both sexes have distinctive long pointed tails.

30

California
Quail

♂

♀

Gambel's
Quail

♂

♀

Ring-necked
Pheasant

♀

♂

DOVES

BAND-TAILED PIGEON

MOURNING DOVE

ROCK DOVE

A flock of band-tailed pigeons flying in the distance can be distinguished from rock doves by their uniformity; rock dove plumages vary.

Doves (or pigeons — there is no difference) can be depended on to show up at backyard feeders. They have very short legs and walk on the ground like gamebirds rather than hopping along like most birds. As they walk, they bob their heads back and forth in a characteristic fashion.

In the wild, where they are declining in some regions, band-tailed pigeons take mostly seeds and acorns. Some venture into parks and backyards for seeds or the berries of ornamental plants. The white bar on the back of the neck and the namesake band of gray on the tip of the **band-tailed pigeon's** tail are sure marks separating it from dark variations of the rock dove.

Mourning doves and rock doves are widespread and abundant. **Mourning doves** are the ones with long pointed tails. A mournful call, *woo-oó-oo, oo, oo, oo,* is given in spring and summer by unmated males.

Rock dove is the formal name for the well-known pigeon of cities and farms. Pigeons have colonized most of the world in the company of man. The many color variations seen are the result of interbreeding with exotic domesticated strains. The ancestral form is shown in the foreground.

32

Band-tailed Pigeon

Mourning Dove

Rock Dove

WOOD-PECKERS

The most common backyard woodpecker is the downy. It is also the smallest, just 7 inches long. The hairy woodpecker has virtually the identical plumage pattern but is 2 inches larger. Some forms of both species may have very few wing spots and/or a brownish gray cast to their white plumage.

DOWNY WOODPECKER

HAIRY WOODPECKER

The size difference is easy to recognize when the two species are seen side by side, but can be hard to judge when the birds are seen separately. The best mark is the bill length. The **hairy woodpecker** has a much larger bill — nearly as long as its head. The **downy woodpecker's** bill extends only about half its head length.

The pileated woodpecker is sometimes seen in mature trees in parks or woodlots. It is a large, mostly black bird the size of a crow, with a pointed, flaming red crest and white patches in its wings.

Males of both species have a bright red patch on the back of their crowns that is lacking in females. Young birds of both sexes also show a patch of red on their heads, but the color is more diffuse and is located on the center or forepart of the crown rather than on the rear.

There is a very small plumage difference that can be noted at close range on most birds. The hairy's white outer tail feathers are unmarked, while the downy's are marked with two or more black bars.

young

hairy

Downy
Woodpecker

♀

♂

♀

Hairy
Woodpecker

♂

WOOD-PECKERS

LADDER-BACKED WOODPECKER

RED-SHAFTED FLICKER

ACORN WOODPECKER

Nuttall's woodpecker replaces the ladder-backed in parts of California. The only notable differences are in the black and white face pattern.

The woodpeckers shown on these pages seldom show up at suet or seed feeders. The red-shafted flicker is usually seen on the ground in open short-grass areas such as lawns or parks, where it feeds on ants, its favorite meal. Like other woodpeckers, flickers gather insects from trees, but because they often feed on the ground, they are sometimes not recognized as woodpeckers.

The typical view of a **red-shafted flicker** is of a white-rumped bird rising in flight from the ground and flying directly away, flashing red in the underwing. Seen closer, the flicker has strikingly patterned plumage. The male has a red mustache mark lacking in females.

Ladder-backed woodpeckers are common in residential areas of the desert Southwest. They nest and feed in cactus as well as trees. The **ladder-backed woodpecker** is the same size as the similar downy woodpecker on the previous page, but has horizontal bars on its back instead of a white vertical stripe.

Acorn woodpeckers are common in parks and suburbs, usually in small noisy groups. They drill holes in trees (sometimes in buildings) for storage of acorns. **Acorn woodpeckers** are unmistakable. The red on the crown of the female is more restricted than in the male.

Ladder-backed
Woodpecker

♀

♂

Red-shafted Flicker

♂

Acorn Woodpecker

♀

♂

NUTHATCHES AND CREEPER

WHITE-BREASTED NUTHATCH

RED-BREASTED NUTHATCH

BROWN CREEPER

The pygmy nuthatch is found in pine forest. It is just a bit smaller than the red-breasted and is distinguished by its gray-brown cap and pale spot on its hind neck.

Not all birds seen climbing a tree trunk are woodpeckers. Nuthatches and the brown creeper also make a living on the insects and larvae hidden in a tree's bark. Nuthatches are the only tree-climbers so agile that they can creep *down* a tree. Presumably they find morsels that upward-climbers miss. They also forage for insects at the tips of small branches and take seeds from pine cones.

The **white-breasted nuthatch** is the most common nuthatch at most feeders. It is dark above and white below with an inconspicuous wash of rusty red on its flanks. Females are the same as males, except some are notice-ably grayer on the crown.

Red-breasted nuthatches prefer conifers. They are smaller than the white-breasted, have a rusty-red breast and belly, and sport a white stripe above the eye. Females are noticeably duller than males.

The **brown creeper** is often overlooked. It can appear on the trunk of any tree, especially mature ones, and blends into the background of bark. It spirals up a tree trunk searching for insects and is often not noticed until it flies from one tree to the base of another.

White-breasted
Nuthatch

♀

Red-
breasted
Nuthatch

♂

Brown Creeper

FLYCATCHER AND KINGBIRDS

ASH-THROATED FLYCATCHER

WESTERN KINGBIRD

EASTERN KINGBIRD

Cassin's kingbird can also be recognized by its call, a rough, nasal *che-bew.* Western kingbirds give a single sharp note, *kip!*

Eastern and western kingbirds are fly-catchers like the ash-throated flycatcher shown here and the phoebes on the following pages. All wait patiently on an open perch for an insect to pass by. After catching the bug midair, the flycatcher often returns to the same perch to repeat the process. Flycatchers are tolerant of people and tend to gather wherever flying insects are available.

Kingbirds are particularly conspicuous because of their noisy, aggressive behavior. The white-tipped tail is the sure mark for the **eastern kingbird,** which actually ranges a bit farther west in Canada than the western kingbird.

Western kingbirds and **ash-throated fly-catchers** look similar but have differences. Note the pale throat and upper breast of the western kingbird and the white edges to its black tail. The ash-throated flycatcher flashes a rusty red in its wings and tail when it flies.

The western kingbird has an even closer look-alike, Cassin's kingbird, which lives in the high, open lands of Arizona, New Mexico, Utah, Wyoming, and Colorado. There is also a pop-ulation in California's coastal foothills. Cassin's is darker gray than the western, making the white throat appear more prominent. Its tail lacks white edges and has a dusky tip.

40

Ash-throated
Flycatcher

Western
Kingbird

Eastern Kingbird

CEDAR WAXWING

SAY'S PHOEBE

BLACK PHOEBE

Vermilion flycatchers are common in parts of the Southwest. The male is vermilion and black; the female a bit like Say's phoebe but has a white throat and streaked breast.

Waxwings wander in flocks of up to a hundred birds or so except when nesting. They keep in close contact, giving a pleasing high-pitched, lisping call. A flock of these sleek birds will often sit awhile in the top of a tall tree before flying down to feed on fruit or berries. They also catch insects, flycatcher fashion, in summer.

The tiny dots of red on its wings are the source of the waxwing's name. They suggest the wax once used for sealing documents. The crest, narrow dark mask, and yellow tail tip are the easiest marks for identifying the **cedar waxwing**.

Both the black phoebe and Say's phoebe are common and tame around buildings. The black phoebe is especially attracted to water. It often flycatches from a low perch, capturing bugs close to the ground. The black upperparts and white belly of the **black phoebe** might suggest a junco (p. 80) at first glance, but the two birds don't feed or behave at all like each other.

Say's phoebe prefers arid habitats in summer, where it sometimes flycatches from a boulder when a fence or bush is not available. The combination of tawny underparts and unstreaked gray throat is distinctive for **Say's phoebe.**

42

Cedar Waxwing

young

Say's Phoebe

Black Phoebe

THRASHER AND WRENS

CALIFORNIA THRASHER

HOUSE WREN

BEWICK'S WREN

The most common thrasher of the Southwest is the curve-billed thrasher. It has blurry breast spots.

A few birds have curved bills that they use to probe for bugs. Thrashers use their bills to rake the soil and leaf litter under shrubs and bushes for insects. Because they are shy and often hidden, thrashers are frequently heard picking through the debris under a bush before they are seen. When surprised, they run or fly low and swiftly into a nearby bush.

The most common thrasher is the **California thrasher.** It is chocolate brown above, russet under the tail, and has a faint white eyebrow. Other thrashers (several species occur in the Southwest) are grayer backed and lack the eyebrow; some have breast spots.

Wrens are not likely to be confused with other birds, even if their slightly curved bill is not noticed. No other small gray-brown bird has similar fine barring on its wings and tail, and none cock their tail or scold so expressively.

Both Bewick's and house wrens are familiar in brushy residential neighborhoods; Bewick's is a bit larger. **House wrens** have a faint eyebrow at best, whereas **Bewick's wren** has a prominent white eyebrow. Bewick's also has white corners in its tail and is whiter below than the house wren. The grayer form of Bewick's is the one seen in the West.

44

California Thrasher

House Wren

Bewick's Wren

gray form

brown form

MOCKINGBIRD AND MAGPIE

MOCKINGBIRD

BLACK-BILLED MAGPIE

One bird, the logger-head shrike, resembles the mockingbird. It is not seen in back-yards but can be found sometimes on roadside fences or wires in open country.

The loggerhead shrike has a shorter bill, a black mask, and a different pattern of white in its wings.

One of the most common and familiar birds in its range, the mockingbird will perch conspicuously on wires, limbs, or often a TV antenna and serenade tirelessly throughout the year, even into the night. It is a famous mimic and will repeat grating, mechanical sounds as readily as the songs of other birds. When perched, the **mockingbird** is a slim gray bird with mostly dark wings and a long, dark tail that it often holds erect. When it takes flight, the white in the wings becomes a prominent mark.

Magpies usually occur in small noisy flocks and are common in rural communities and over farm and range land, especially along streams. They are closely related to jays and crows and, like them, feed on whatever is available, including seeds, insects, and small rodents. Magpies make large, conspicuous, domed nests in trees or shrubs.

The **black-billed magpie's** streaming, dark green, iridescent tail is as strikingly obvious as its black-and-white plumage pattern. Its high, whining *mahg?* call is also distinctive. West of the Sierra Nevada in California, magpies have yellow bills and yellow eye patches and are considered a different species, the yellow-billed magpie.

46

young

Mockingbird

loggerhead
shrike

mockingbird

Black-billed Magpie

RAVENS AND CROWS

AMERICAN CROW

COMMON RAVEN

The great-tailed grackle is increasingly common in the Southwest. Males are large all-black birds with very large tails.

Crows and their larger relatives, ravens, are the most intelligent North American birds. It is an opinion rooted in Native American folklore and confirmed by present-day ornithologists. Crows and ravens are not restricted to a specific diet but will take whatever is available. Their adaptability has permitted them to flourish. Crows are found everywhere except in deserts, mountain forests, and the Arctic. And ravens manage to live year-round even in northernmost Alaska.

Scientists recognize two crow species in the West, the American crow and the northwestern crow. The two species are virtually indistinguishable in the field. Those crows found on the Pacific coast from Puget Sound to Alaska are considered to be northwestern crows.

Separating the much larger **common raven** from the **American crow** is usually just a matter of estimating size and noting tail shape. However, there is the Chihuahuan raven that is about the size of a large crow or a small raven and can be confused with either. It is often found in large flocks at farms and dumps in winter, but only in the Southwest north to southeast Colorado and east to central Texas. Crows give a distinctive *caw* or *cah*. Ravens have a hoarse, low-pitched *c-r-ock* call, higher in the Chihuahuan raven.

American Crow

Common Raven

PINYON JAY

WESTERN SCRUB-JAY

STELLER'S JAY

If you are camping in northern conifers, chances are your "backyard" bird is a gray jay (gray, crestless, small bill). These fearless "camprobbers" boldy steal from tent and table.

Scrub-jays and Steller's jays boldly come to backyard feeders for seeds in all seasons. Pinyon jays are much rarer, primarily winter, visitors to neighborhoods and backyard feeders.

Most jays, including Steller's and scrub-jays, are slim birds with long tails. However, the pinyon jay is shaped like a small crow. It behaves and flies like one as well and is often found in large flocks. The sky-blue plumage of the **pinyon jay** is darkest on the head. The throat is gray with fine blue streaks.

The bird widely known as a scrub jay is now believed to be several species. The widespread western species has been named the western scrub-jay. The intensity of the **western scrub-jay's** blues and grays varies regionally, but the pattern remains the same. Scrub-jays store acorns for winter and are well known for taking bright trinkets and adding them to their cache.

The prominent crest and black foreparts are easy marks for identifying **Steller's jay.** The streaks on the eyebrow, chin, and crest vary regionally. They can be blue or white or may even be absent. Steller's jay is also likely to be seen in the conifers of a park or woodlot, where it feeds primarily on nuts and seeds.

50

young

Pinyon Jay

Western
Scrub-jay

Steller's Jay

young

PARK

STARLING AND COWBIRD

STARLING

BROWN-HEADED COWBIRD

The bronzed cowbird is found in parts of the Southwest. It has red eyes and a noticeably larger bill than the brown-headed.

Both starlings and cowbirds are a serious threat to other western species. Originally introduced from Europe to the New York area, the starling rapidly spread across the United States and southern Canada. It nests in cavities and has displaced native cavity-nesters such as the western bluebird (p. 60), purple martin, and Lewis' woodpecker.

The **starling's** plumage varies by season from spotted to glossy black. The birds have short tails and long pointed bills. The **brown-headed cowbird's** best mark is its conical bill. (The bird is illustrated here rather than with other conically billed birds because it most resembles a blackbird.) Males are black with a dark brown head; females, a dull gray-brown.

Cowbirds were originally birds of the Great Plains and were then known as "buffalo birds." They spread across the continent as man converted forest to farmland. Cowbirds are nest parasites. They lay an egg in other birds' nests, and the host birds raise the cowbird chick, usually at the expense of their own young. The cowbird's threat to some species is so serious that many bird conservationists give the problem top priority. However, the bird did not create the problem. We created it by altering the landscape.

52

young

fall

Starling

spring

molting young ♂
in fall

**Brown-headed
Cowbird**

♀

♂

BLACKBIRDS

YELLOW-HEADED BLACKBIRD

BREWER'S BLACKBIRD

RED-WINGED BLACKBIRD

Male great-tailed grackles might be confused with Brewer's blackbird. See the sidebar on p. 48.

All the blackbirds live in flocks. In winter, they are frequently seen in mixed flocks that can include cowbirds and starlings. Only red-winged and Brewer's blackbirds are common at feeding stations.

Yellow-headed blackbirds nest in freshwater marshlands and feed in nearby fields and farmlands. Male and female **yellow-headed blackbirds** are strikingly different, with the female being smaller, browner, and showing yellow only on her throat and breast.

Preferring fields to marshes, Brewer's blackbird has spread across much of the continent as ranching and dairy farming have created its preferred habitat. It is now the most commonly seen blackbird in the West and can be found in parking lots as well as backyards. Male **Brewer's blackbirds** have yellow eyes and a metallic sheen that shows in good light. Females are gray-brown with dark eyes.

It is the male **red-winged blackbird** that is usually seen in backyards; females are shier. Females look like big streaked sparrows but have a blackbird's bill. The male's orange-red shoulders are often hidden with only the buff edges showing. The buff is absent in birds of California's Central Valley.

54

Yellow-headed
Blackbird

♀

♂

Brewer's
Blackbird

♂

♀

Red-winged Blackbird

♂

♀

ORIOLE AND MEADOWLARK

BULLOCK'S ORIOLE

WESTERN MEADOWLARK

Hooded orioles come to nectar feeders, especially in the Southwest, and Scott's oriole might be seen in ornamental growth.

The male Scott's is black and yellow, including a black hood. The male hooded is yellow to orange with black markings, including a distinctive solid black tail — but no hood.

Although more brightly colored than blackbirds, meadowlarks and orioles belong to the same family as blackbirds. The most telling similarity is bill shape.

Orioles visit parks, orchards, and residential shade trees. They sometimes visit backyard feeding stations for orange halves or a sugar-water feeder like that set out for hummingbirds. The nest of a Bullock's oriole is a conspicuous, large oval bag, often attached to the twigs on the outer branch of a large shade tree.

Male and female **Bullock's orioles** have different plumages. The adult male is bright and distinctive; note especially the large white wing patch. Females and yearling males lack the wing patch and the warm orange tones on the face and body. They are yellow on the face, breast, and under the tail, blending to pale gray on the belly. The yearling male has a black throat and eyeline.

The **western meadowlark** is well known for its black V on a bright yellow breast. It is a common roadside bird, often perching on posts or wires to deliver its rich, flute-like song. The white in the tail is also a good mark as it flies away on stiff wings with shallow strokes and short glides.

56

young ♂

Bullock's Oriole

♀

♂

Western Meadowlark

winter

summer

WESTERN TANAGER

ROBIN

Summer tanagers of the Southwest are shaped like western tanagers, but males are bright red overall. Females lack the western tanager's wing bars.

The varied thrush is a relative of the robin found in moist coniferous forests. Males are orange below and have black breast bands.

Western tanagers are not common in residential areas, but they are regular spring migrants and summer visitors in shade trees. More are not seen because they are relatively slow-moving birds that often stay hidden in the canopy of mature trees.

The male **western tanager** is spectacular in his brilliant summer plumage, but by fall he begins to molt to a female-like yellow-green dress. His wings and tail remain black, however, distinguishing him from the female.

The plumage of the female western tanager is much like that of the female oriole, greenish yellow below and olive gray above with two wing bars. Shape, especially bill shape, is the best mark separating the two. The tanager is more compact; its bill is shorter and more swollen than the long pointed bill of the oriole.

One of the first birds a child learns to recognize is the robin. But how many people ever notice that female **robins** are distinctively paler gray above and paler orange below than males? Young birds are heavily spotted.

The songs of both birds are somewhat similar: whistled flute-like notes given in short phrases. The tanager's song has a burrier tone.

spring ♂

♀

Western Tanager

young

Robin

CATBIRD

MOUNTAIN BLUEBIRD

WESTERN BLUEBIRD

The lazuli bunting often visits weedy fields. It suggests a western bluebird at first glance, but note the seed-crusher bill and the wing bars.

The catbird is a skulker, much more common in the bushes and thickets of backyards and parks than many bird watchers suspect. Its name comes from a cat-like mewing that it often makes. The only distinctive marks on the plain gray **catbird** are the rusty patch under the base of the tail, which is hard to see, and the black cap.

Both mountain and western bluebirds use boxes for nesting, as well as hollows in trees. There is much competition for nest sites with starlings (p. 52), house sparrows (p. 84), and tree swallows (p. 26).

Mountain bluebirds range from foothills to the treeline. They flycatch but more often perch or hover over open ground and flutter down to capture ground insects. Blue in the female **mountain bluebird** is limited to the rump, tail, and wings. Males are truly blue.

The female **western bluebird** is paler than the impressive male, with bright blue only in the wings and tail. The blue is palest in young birds, which also have spotting on their backs and breasts. Family groups are often seen together throughout the summer in parks and suburbs. Western bluebirds capture bugs on the ground, much as mountain bluebirds do.

60

Catbird

♀

♂
Mountain
Bluebird

♀
Western
Bluebird

♂

WARBLERS

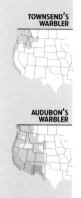

TOWNSEND'S
WARBLER

AUDUBON'S
WARBLER

Audubon's warbler
and the myrtle war-
bler are now consid-
ered the same species
by ornithologists, who
call it the yellow-
rumped warbler.

The myrtle warbler
nests in the North
and occurs in small
numbers in the West
in winter and
migration. Its most
obvious difference
from Audubon's is its
white throat.

➢

Eighteen different kinds of warblers —
each more beautiful than the other —
nest in or migrate through western North
America. Almost any of them might conceiv-
ably choose your backyard for a brief layover.
Audubon's warbler is one of the most likely
visitors; Townsend's warbler is more likely to
be seen at a park, especially in conifers.

To identify any warbler, begin by noting
whether or not it shows yellow and whether
or not it has wing bars. If you get these
two marks first and then note other prominent features, you will have the best chance
of success.

Audubon's and Townsend's warblers show
yellow and have wing bars. **Townsend's
warbler** has yellow concentrated on the face
and breast. Spring males have a black crown,
eye patch, and bib. These markings are duller
in females and young birds, both of which
lack the bib.

All plumages of **Audubon's warbler** have
a yellow rump. There are also distinctive
patches of yellow on the throat and on the
side near the shoulder, although sometimes
faint on young birds in fall. Spring males have
a yellow crown. Audubon's warbler is widespread and abundant, even in winter.

spring ♂

♀

Townsend's Warbler

Audubon's Warbler

young

spring ♂

spring ♀

WARBLERS

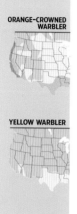

ORANGE-CROWNED WARBLER

YELLOW WARBLER

Yellow and orange-crowned warblers may also be separated by their song and call notes.

The yellow warbler has a sweet song and a rich *chip* call. The orange-crowned's song is a thin trill; its call, a metallic *chip*.

Two of the most common and widespread warblers in the West are the orange-crowned and the yellow warblers. Both frequent bushes, shrubs, and the lower limbs of trees and are conspicuous. They are likely to be seen in residential neighborhoods, especially if there is water nearby.

Orange-crowned and yellow warblers show yellow but have no wing bars. At their plumage extremes, the two species should not be confused. The **yellow warbler** is virtually all yellow. Males are bright and have chestnut breast streaks. The identification problem occurs among some of the duller fall females.

As in many warblers, the plumage of the yellow warbler varies with sex, age, and season. A young yellow warbler in fall can be greenish and duller than some orange-crowned warblers. On dull yellow warblers, look for the beady dark eye and the yellow edges on their wing feathers that give the wings a striped effect. Another good mark is the yellow eye-ring, which becomes noticeable on dull birds. In flight, the yellow tail spots are visible.

Most **orange-crowned warblers** are nondescript olive-yellow birds with only a thin broken eye-ring and a faint eyeline. This plainness is, in fact, their best mark.

64

Orange-crowned Warbler

Yellow Warbler

WARBLERS

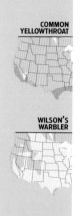

COMMON YELLOWTHROAT

WILSON'S WARBLER

Yellowthroats are often skulkers except when the male is claiming a territory, openly singing his *wichity, wichity, wichity* song. Also listen for the species' low, husky *chuf* call.

Wilson's warbler and the yellowthroat show yellow and lack wing bars. Both are especially attracted to water. Wilson's is bold and active, picking bugs from foliage and often flycatching. It is likely to be seen in small or medium-sized trees.

The yellowthroat is more secretive but is still often seen in the open. The yellowthroat forages at lower levels in brush and bushes. It behaves a bit like a wren — very active, scolding, and then disappearing in dense brush or briars. Marsh edges and the moister portions of fields are its favorite nesting habitats.

Male **Wilson's warblers** and **common yellowthroats** are distinctively patterned. As with most warblers, it is the females and young birds that present identification problems. The crown of the female Wilson's is always dark, if not as black as the male's. Wilson's also has the distinctive habit of flicking its relatively long tail and holding it cocked expressively.

Best mark for the female yellowthroat is a subtle one. Note how the yellow under the tail and on the breast blends to a brownish gray on the belly. Similar warblers are yellow from breast to tail.

Common Yellowthroat

♂

♀

young ♂

Wilson's
Warbler

♀

♂

CHICKADEES AND TITMICE

OAK AND JUNIPER TITMICE

BLACK-CAPPED CHICKADEE

CHESTNUT-BACKED CHICKADEE

MOUNTAIN CHICKADEE

Some of the boldest and also most welcome birds at backyard feeders are the chickadees and the titmice. The birds are closely related and have similar habits. During the summer, they feed mostly on insects and visit feeders infrequently. In winter, they eat seeds and nuts and regularly attend backyard feeders.

Perky crests distinguish the plain gray **titmice.** Coastal birds are a little browner than interior ones and are now considered a separate species. Coastal birds are called oak titmice; interior ones, juniper titmice.

Black-capped chickadees, with their buff sides and black caps and throats, are the most widespread and likely chickadee visitors to most feeders within their range.

Chestnut-backed chickadees are common in residential areas and feeding stations in the Pacific Coast states. In some California birds, the sides can be gray with little or no chestnut.

Mountain chickadees are common at high elevations in summer. Some appear at low-land feeders in winter. **Mountain chickadees** are distinguished by their white eyebrow and gray sides.

68

Oak and
Juniper
Titmice

Black-capped
Chickadee

Chestnut-backed
Chickadee

Mountain Chickadee

BUSHTIT AND KINGLETS

BUSHTIT

RUBY-CROWNED KINGLET

GOLDEN-CROWNED KINGLET

The tiny bushtit and kinglets are the smallest North American songbirds. **Bushtits** are gray-brown and have fairly long tails. Females have pale eyes. Coastal birds have brownish caps, and some interior males in the Southwest have a black patch on the face. When not nesting, bushtits forage in noisy flocks in brush and shrubs from backyards to foothills.

Kinglets are very active birds that nest in coniferous forest and are most often seen in migration and in winter. They visit parks and backyard shrubs and trees but not feeders. The more numerous ruby-crowned kinglet takes a few seeds in winter, but for the most part, kinglets manage to find hidden insect matter even in cold and snowy weather.

The color of their crown and the white eyebrow are good marks for the **golden-crowned kinglet. Ruby-crowned kinglets** are more nondescript; only the male shows red, and it is usually concealed. The tiny bill, plump body, wing-flicking behavior, and short tail distinguish the ruby-crowned from the warblers it might be confused with. The clinching marks are a white eye-ring broken at the top and a white wing bar bordered below by a dark patch — the kinglet patch.

70

black-eared form

coastal ♂

Bushtit

interior ♂

♀

♂

**Ruby-crowned
Kinglet**

♀

**Golden-crowned
Kinglet**

♀

♂

TOWHEES

SPOTTED TOWHEE

CALIFORNIA TOWHEE

Widely known as the rufous-sided towhee, the spotted towhee was renamed in 1995 by ornithologists who decided it and its very similar eastern relatives (now named eastern towhees) were distinct species.

Brush-loving birds with long rounded tails, towhees are common in back-yards, parks, and roadsides, although often hidden. Like the thrashers (p. 44), towhees feed on the ground in the debris and leaf litter under shrubs and bushes. They eat insects as well as seeds.

The rusty-colored sides are good marks for adult **spotted towhees.** Until recently they were called rufous-sided towhees, a much more appropriate and traditional name (see sidebar). Male spotted towhees have black hoods and backs with a variable number of white spots. The black is replaced by gray in adult females. Long black tails with white in the corners are prominent marks in both male and female plumages. Birds just out of the nest are brownish overall and heavily streaked.

The California towhee is especially fond of parks and suburbs. In some suburbs, it is known as the "muffler bird" because of its fondness for hiding under parked cars as if they were brush piles. **California towhees** are dull brown, darker on the tail, paler on the face and throat. There is a hard-to-see patch of rusty color under the tail.

72

Spotted Towhee

California Towhee

GROSBEAKS

BLACK-HEADED GROSBEAK

EVENING GROSBEAK

Pine grosbeaks live in the coniferous forest of the Rockies and Pacific Northwest. The male is red with white wing bars; the female, gray with an olive head and rump.

Big finches with very heavy bills, the grosbeaks are special visitors to backyard feeders. Black-headed grosbeaks visit in spring and are often seen in pairs. They eat insects as much as seeds in summer, so they are seldom regular visitors to a sunflower seed station. Evening grosbeaks gather in wandering flocks and often show up at feeders in winter.

Adult male **black-headed grosbeaks** are a striking butterscotch and black that is easy to identify. Also note the white patches in the wings. The female's plumage resembles that of many smaller finches, but her large bill, wash of buff-yellow on the breast, and distinct eyebrow and crown stripes are good marks. There is some fine streaking below, mainly along the sides. Both male and female show yellow in the underwing in flight.

The male **evening grosbeak** is as distinctive as the male black-headed. The large white wing patches, stubby tail, and yellow forehead and eyebrows are all easily seen marks. Females are much grayer and have smaller white wing patches. Evening grosbeaks are attracted by road salt as well as sunflower seeds. They are relatively tame birds that occur irregularly in fall and winter, numerous one year and absent the next.

74

Black-headed Grosbeak

♂

♀

Evening Grosbeak

♂

♀

GOLDFINCHES AND SISKIN

AMERICAN GOLDFINCH

PINE SISKIN

LESSER GOLDFINCH

Lawrence's goldfinch is scarce and irregular in California and Arizona. It shows a lot of yellow in the wings, but not much on the body. Males have a black face.

Some of the most colorful little seed-crunchers are the goldfinches, especially the male American goldfinch in summer. American goldfinches are easily attracted to backyards by thistle seed feeders. Pine siskins and lesser goldfinches also come to backyards and suburbs, although not as commonly.

Female **American goldfinches** and males in fall and winter are a dull, unstreaked olive brown above. The white under their tails and their pale bills are good marks. Males retain their black wings and tail in winter and also a small but bright yellow shoulder patch. Flocks of goldfinches can be recognized by their distinctive roller-coaster flight.

Male **lesser goldfinches** come in two forms, the numerous green-backed and much scarcer black-backed, with some birds intermediate. Females can be safely distinguished from female American goldfinches by the yellow under their tails.

Although they are in the same genus as goldfinches, **pine siskins** show little yellow except in the spread wing. They have a small, sharply pointed bill for a finch — a small mark but a good one separating them from other brown-striped finches.

76

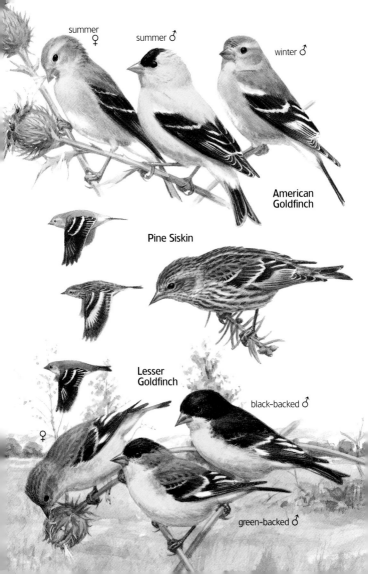

summer ♀

summer ♂

winter ♂

American
Goldfinch

Pine Siskin

Lesser
Goldfinch

black-backed ♂

♀

green-backed ♂

RED FINCHES

HOUSE FINCH

PURPLE FINCH

Cassin's finch visits feeders in mountain yards. Males are like male purple finches, but the red is brightest on the crown. The nape and back are mostly brown.

The female Cassin's has less pronounced white eyebrows and whisker marks than in the female purple finch. The breast streaks are finer and extend under the tail.

Both the purple and house finches can be seen in backyards. House finches tend to be year-round visitors to a feeder; purple finches visit most often in winter. Calling out a purple finch from among a flock of house finches is a good bird-watching challenge.

Males of both species have a splash of red on them that varies considerably among individuals. Distinguishing one species from another requires care. The females are plain, brown-striped birds that require even more care in identification.

House finches are a little slimmer than **purple finches** and have smaller heads and bills. Side by side the difference is perceptible. Male house finches have brown streaking on their sides and bellies that is lacking in purple finches. The red on the male house finch's head is concentrated on the forehead and eyebrows. On the purple finch, the red extends onto the crown, nape, and back and tends to be more wine-colored.

The contrast of the broad white eyebrow and whisker stripe on the female purple finch is her best mark. The face of the female house finch is much plainer; her breast streaks are a bit finer and extend all the way under her less deeply notched tail.

House Finch

Purple Finch

JUNCOS

SLATE-COLORED JUNCO

GRAY-HEADED JUNCO

OREGON JUNCO

The white-winged junco inhabits the ponderosa pines of the Black Hills, South Dakota, and has white wing bars. Otherwise it looks much like the slate-colored junco.

No songbird shows more variation than the junco. Scientists have often reversed themselves on whether the different forms should be classified as species or as races of a single species. Currently all forms are considered races of one species: the dark-eyed junco.

All forms of the **dark-eyed junco** have dark eyes, pale bills, and white outer tail feathers. The white in the tail is especially conspicuous when the bird flies from the ground, where it feeds, to the low branches of a tree.

The slate-colored is the most widespread form of the junco. It is seen during winter and migration in most of the West. Males are slate gray with white bellies. Females are duller, browner, and can show contrast between the hood and the back.

The gray-headed junco of the Rockies and Great Basin has a pale gray head and sides and a rusty-colored back.

The Oregon form is the most numerous in the Pacific Coast states. The male has a black hood, buff to pinkish sides, and a rusty-brown back. Females are duller. In the northern Rockies, Oregon juncos have broader pink sides and a paler hood with a contrasting dark area in front of the eye.

80

♀

♂

Slate-colored
Junco

Gray-headed Junco

♀

Oregon
Junco

Oregon Pink-
sided Junco

CROWNED SPARROWS

GOLDEN-CROWNED SPARROW

WHITE-CROWNED SPARROW

In both golden- and white-crowned sparrows, the young birds just out of the nest have streaked breasts. The streaks don't last long, perhaps a few weeks at most.

P rominent crown stripes distinguish the golden-crowned and white-crowned sparrows. Both are seen on the ground at feeders in backyards, usually in winter or during migration. The two species often flock and feed together in winter, although golden-crowned sparrows are less numerous than white-crowns and less likely visitors to most backyards.

Both **golden-** and **white-crowned sparrows** are large for sparrows. The golden-crowned is slightly the larger and has duskier underparts. In the white-crowned sparrow, the bill is pink to orange. In the golden-crowned, the upper mandible is dusky; the lower one, pale. These minor points can be useful in identifying some young birds in a mixed flock.

Young birds are not as readily identifiable as the unmistakable adults. Young golden-crowns usually show at least a hint of the adult's crown pattern and color (on the forehead), but it requires imagination to see it at times. Young white-crowned sparrows have brown crown stripes.

Gambel's form of the white-crowned is the most common subspecies in many areas. Its black eyeline stops at the eye instead of continuing in front to the bill. Some coastal birds are browner than those shown.

82

Golden-crowned Sparrow

young

very young late summer

White-crowned Sparrow

Gambel's form

young

very young late summer

DISTINCTIVE SPARROWS

LARK SPARROW

HOUSE SPARROW

Although not common in the West, the tree sparrow can be confused with the lark sparrow. It, too, has a dark breast spot and some rusty or chestnut color on its head. However, it is smaller, slimmer, and has no black head markings or white tail corners.

Lark sparrows tolerate civilization; house sparrows embrace it, abundantly. Winter is the best time to find lark sparrows feeding on the ground in a backyard or local park. Normally birds of open woodlands and grassy areas, they have adapted to roadsides and farmlands. They are very social, living and foraging in small flocks except when nesting.

Lark sparrows have a number of good marks: an elaborate head pattern, white corners in the tail, and a dark spot in the center of a plain breast. The young birds, which are usually seen with adults, have a much less prominent head pattern. Fresh from the nest, the young show a few breast streaks.

House sparrows were introduced to New York from Europe in 1851. After years of expanding their range and numbers, they now blanket the United States and are actually beginning to decline in some areas, although perhaps not at your feeder. Male **house sparrows** have a black bib and chestnut head markings. In fresh plumage (fall), these marks are partially obscured. The female house sparrow is quite plain. Her only good marks are the plain underparts, the pale eyebrow, and the pale bill.

84

very young
late summer

Lark Sparrow

fall ♂

House Sparrow

♀

spring ♂

SPARROWS

CHIPPING SPARROW

FOX SPARROW

The tree sparrow is closely related to the chipping sparrow, and the two are similar enough to be confused. See the sidebar on page 84.

The chipping sparrow is one of of the smallest sparrows; the fox sparrow, one of the largest. The little chippies are common park and neighborhood birds in summer. They spend more time feeding on lawns, roadsides, and unpaved driveways than they do at feeding stations. In winter, most migrate to the Southwest or out of the United States.

In summer, the **chipping sparrow** has a distinctive rusty crown, a white eyebrow, and a black eyeline that extends through the eye to the bill. Winter birds are harder to identify, but the dark eyeline through the eye together with the gray rump distinguishes it from similar sparrows.

Fox sparrows are regular in residential areas, but they like brush for cover and don't often come out to feed in the open at a feeding station. They are more numerous in brushy canyons and hillsides.

The several western races of the **fox sparrow** show substantial plumage variation, but all have heavy streaking below, which often merges into a central breast spot. The tail is a particularly good mark. Long and blunt (not rounded like the song sparrow's), it is usually rusty red, but some very dark birds have few reddish tones in the tail.

variations

Fox Sparrow

Chipping Sparrow

very young
late summer

first winter

summer

STREAKED SPARROWS

LINCOLN'S
SPARROW

SONG SPARROW

SAVANNAH
SPARROW

The vesper sparrow can be seen on road-sides or in dry short-grass fields. It has a streaked breast, white eye-ring, and slightly notched tail with white outer feathers.

Brown streaking on the breast is an important mark for many sparrows. Not all birds with streaked breasts are sparrows, however. See the female red-winged blackbird (p. 54), young cowbird (p. 52), finches (p. 78), and pine siskin (p. 76).

Song sparrows are fairly common in backyards, more numerous in brushy parks or streamsides. Lincoln's and savannah sparrows are wary and more reluctant to come out from cover. Lincoln's sparrows like brushy areas in winter. Savannah sparrows are seen in open grassy roadsides, agricultural fields, and parks.

The center breast spot that is often used to identify **song sparrows** is not a conclusive mark; fox sparrows (p. 86) have it, and so do many savannahs and some Lincoln's sparrows. The song sparrow's heavy black whisker mark and long rounded tail should also be noted. **Lincoln's sparrow** is similar to the song sparrow but is smaller, and the breast and the area below the cheek are buff; also note the finer breast streaking and whisker mark.

Savannah sparrows have a short notched tail and usually a fainter whisker mark than the song sparrow has. Many are paler overall than the song sparrow, and some have a yellow spot before the eye.

88

Lincoln's Sparrow

Song Sparrow

young

Savannah Sparrow

typical

dark

Sooner or later all bird-watchers, even the most casual, wonder how many different species they have seen or how many have visited their backyard. Keeping a record is the only way to know. A list of species seen can become part of the pleasure of bird-watching.

Your backyard list can be put to scientific use by the Cornell Lab of Ornithology. Their Project FeederWatch, begun in 1987 as a joint US-Canadian project with Bird Studies Canada, compiles the counts of backyard birders. Participants receive a research kit and a quarterly newsletter of feeder-watch results for a low annual fee. For more information, call 1-800-843-2473 (1-519-586-3531 in Canada).

✓ Species	Date	Location
◯ BREWER'S **B**LACKBIRD 54 *Euphagus cyanocephalus*[1]	....	....
◯ RED–WINGED **B**LACKBIRD 54 *Agelaius phoeniceus*	....	....
◯ YELLOW–HEADED **B**LACKBIRD 54 *Xanthocephalus xanthocephalus*	....	....
◯ MOUNTAIN **B**LUEBIRD 60 *Sialia currucoides*	....	....
◯ WESTERN **B**LUEBIRD 60 *Sialia mexicana*	....	....
◯ **B**USHTIT 70 *Psaltriparus minimus*	....	....
◯ **C**ATBIRD 60 Gray Catbird[2] *Dumetella carolinensis*	....	....

[1] Names in *italics* are the scientific names adopted by the American Ornithologists' Union.
[2] When the AOU English name differs from the common name as used in this guide, the official AOU English name is given on the second line.

✓ Species	Date	Location

⬤ BLACK-CAPPED **C**HICKADEE 68
Parus atricapillus

⬤ CHESTNUT-BACKED **C**HICKADEE 68
Parus rufescens

⬤ CALIFORNIA **C**ONDOR 20
Gymnogyps californianus

⬤ BROWN-HEADED **C**OWBIRD 52
Molothrus ater

⬤ BROWN **C**REEPER 38
Certhia americana

⬤ AMERICAN **C**ROW 48
Corvus brachyrhynchos

⬤ MOURNING **D**OVE 32
Zenaida macroura

⬤ ROCK **D**OVE 32
Columba livia

⬤ HOUSE **F**INCH 78
Carpodacus mexicanus

⬤ PURPLE **F**INCH 78
Carpodacus purpureus

⬤ RED-SHAFTED **F**LICKER 36
Northern Flicker
Colaptes auratus

⬤ ASH-THROATED **F**LYCATCHER 40
Myiarchus cinerascens

⬤ AMERICAN **G**OLDFINCH 76
Carduelis tristis

⬤ LESSER **G**OLDFINCH 76
Carduelis psaltria

⬤ BLACK-HEADED **G**ROSBEAK 74
Pheucticus melanocephalus

⬤ EVENING **G**ROSBEAK 74
Coccothraustes vespertinus

⬤ COOPER'S **H**AWK 24
Accipiter cooperii

✓ Species		Date	Location

◯	RED-TAILED HAWK *Buteo jamaicensis*	22	....	....
◯	SHARP-SHINNED HAWK *Accipiter striatus*	24	....	....
◯	ANNA'S HUMMINGBIRD *Calypte anna*	28	....	....
◯	BLACK-CHINNED HUMMINGBIRD *Archilochus alexandri*	28	....	....
◯	BROAD-TAILED HUMMINGBIRD *Selasphorus platycercus*	28	....	....
◯	RUFOUS HUMMINGBIRD *Selasphorus rufus*	28	....	....
◯	PINYON JAY *Gymnorhinus cyanocephalus*	50	....	....
	WESTERN SCRUB-JAY *see SCRUB-JAY*			
◯	STELLER'S JAY *Cyanocitta stelleri*	50	....	....
◯	DARK-EYED JUNCO *Junco hyemalis*	80	....	....
◯	KESTREL American Kestrel *Falco sparverius*	22	....	....
◯	EASTERN KINGBIRD *Tyrannus tyrannus*	40	....	....
◯	WESTERN KINGBIRD *Tyrannus verticalis*	40	....	....
◯	GOLDEN-CROWNED KINGLET *Regulus satrapa*	70	....	....
◯	RUBY-CROWNED KINGLET *Regulus calendula*	70	....	....
◯	BLACK-BILLED MAGPIE *Pica pica*	46	....	....
◯	WESTERN MEADOWLARK *Sturnella neglecta*	56	....	....

✓ Species	Date	Location

MOCKINGBIRD   46
Northern Mockingbird
Mimus polyglottos

COMMON **N**IGHTHAWK   18
Chordeiles minor

RED–BREASTED **N**UTHATCH 38
Sitta canadensis

WHITE–BREASTED **N**UTHATCH 38
Sitta carolinensis

BULLOCK'S **O**RIOLE   56
Icterus bullockii

BARN **O**WL   18
Tyto alba

GREAT HORNED **O**WL   18
Bubo virginianus

RING–NECKED **P**HEASANT   30
Phasianus colchicus

BLACK **P**HOEBE   42
Sayornis nigricans

SAY'S **P**HOEBE   42
Sayornis saya

PIGEON
see ROCK **D**OVE

BAND–TAILED **P**IGEON   32
Columba fasciata

CALIFORNIA **Q**UAIL   30
Callipepla californicus

GAMBEL'S **Q**UAIL   30
Callipepla gambelii

COMMON **R**AVEN   48
Corvus corax

ROBIN   58
American robin
Turdus migratorius

WESTERN **S**CRUB–JAY   50
Aphelocoma californica

✓ Species	Date	Location

○ PINE **S**ISKIN　76
Carduelis pinus

○ CHIPPING **S**PARROW　86
Spizella passerina

○ FOX **S**PARROW　86
Passerella iliaca

○ GOLDEN-CROWNED **S**PARROW　82
Zonotrichia atricapilla

○ HOUSE **S**PARROW　84
Passer domesticus

○ LARK **S**PARROW　84
Chondestes grammacus

○ LINCOLN'S **S**PARROW　88
Melospiza lincolnii

○ SAVANNAH **S**PARROW　88
Passerculus sandwichensis

○ SONG **S**PARROW　88
Melospiza melodia

○ WHITE-CROWNED **S**PARROW　82
Zonotrichia leucophrys

○ **S**TARLING　52
European Starling
Sturnus vulgaris

○ BARN **S**WALLOW　26
Hirundo rustica

○ CLIFF **S**WALLOW　26
Hirundo pyrrhonota

○ TREE **S**WALLOW　26
Tachycineta bicolor

○ WESTERN **T**ANAGER　58
Piranga ludoviciana

○ CALIFORNIA **T**HRASHER　44
Toxostoma redivivum

○ JUNIPER **T**ITMOUSE　68
Baeolophus ridgwayi

☑ **Species**		**Date**	**Location**
○ OAK **T**ITMOUSE *Baeolophus inornatus*	68	....	....
○ CALIFORNIA **T**OWHEE *Pipilo crissalis*	72	....	....
○ SPOTTED **T**OWHEE *Pipilo maculatus*	72	....	....
○ TURKEY **V**ULTURE *Cathartes aura*	20	....	....
○ AUDUBON'S **W**ARBLER Yellow-rumped Warbler *Dendroica coronata*	62	....	....
○ ORANGE-CROWNED **W**ARBLER *Vermivora celata*	64	....	....
○ TOWNSEND'S **W**ARBLER *Dendroica townsendi*	62	....	....
○ WILSON'S **W**ARBLER *Wilsonia pusilla*	66	....	....
○ YELLOW **W**ARBLER *Dendroica petechia*	64	....	....
○ CEDAR **W**AXWING *Bombycilla cedrorum*	42	....	....
○ ACORN **W**OODPECKER *Melanerpes formicivorus*	36	....	....
○ DOWNY **W**OODPECKER *Picoides pubescens*	34	....	....
○ HAIRY **W**OODPECKER *Picoides villosus*	34	....	....
○ LADDER-BACKED **W**OODPECKER *Picoides scalaris*	36	....	....
○ BEWICK'S **W**REN *Thryomanes bewickii*	44	....	....
○ HOUSE **W**REN *Troglodytes aedon*	44	....	....
○ COMMON **Y**ELLOWTHROAT *Geothlypsis trichas*	66	....	....

An American Bird Conservancy
Compact Guide

Paul Lehman
Ornithological Editor

American Bird Conservancy (ABC) is a U.S.-based, not-for-profit organization whose mission is to conserve wild birds and their habitats throughout the Americas. It is the only U.S.-based group dedicated solely to addressing the greatest threats facing birds in the Western Hemisphere. A growing human population is critically impacting bird populations through habitat destruction, direct mortality from such harmful practices as the unwise use of pesticides, and the introduction of invasive species, including free-roaming domestic animals. ABC believes adequate resources exist to overcome these threats and that unifying people, organizations, and agencies around common approaches to priority issues is the key to success.

ABC draws on people and organizations through bird conservation networks—including the North American Bird Conservation Initiative, Partners in Flight, the ABC Policy Council, and ABC's growing international network—to address the most critical issues affecting birds. It builds partnerships of conservation groups, scientists, and the public to tackle these conservation priorities, one by one, using the best skills and expertise available. The key to ABC's unique approach lies in supporting and facilitating these networks without controlling them, establishing consensus on priorities using the best science available, developing collaborative solutions, and then openly sharing credit for successes with its partners. ABC measures its success in terms of changes on the ground for the benefit of target species, populations, and habitats.

ABC members receive *Bird Conservation*, the magazine providing in-depth coverage of American bird conservation by all agencies and groups, and *Bird Calls*, the newsletter covering the full range of bird conservation issues and activities.

For more information, please see these websites:

ABC and the ABC Council: *www.abcbirds.org*
North American Bird Conservation Initiative:
www.nabci.org
North American Waterbird Conservation Plan:
www.nacwcp.org
North American Waterfowl Management Plan:
www.nawmp.ca
Partners in Flight: *www.partnersinflight.org*
United States Shorebird Conservation Plan:
www.manomet.org/USSCP/index.htm

ALL THE

BACKYARD

BIRDS

E A S T

BY JACK L. GRIGGS

HarperResource
An Imprint of HarperCollinsPublishers

Barn Owl

Dedicated to Jack L. Griggs Sr.

Designed by Jack L. Griggs & Peg Alrich
Edited by Virginia Croft
Illustrations reformatted by Jack E. Griggs
from the original illustrations published in
All the Birds of North America
by the following artists:

F. P. Bennett p. 29 (bottom); John Dawson pp. 41–47,
49 (top and center), 75, 77; Dale Dyer pp. 79–89; Larry McQueen pp. 61–73;
Hans Peeters pp. 19–25, 31, 33, 49 (bottom), 51–59; Doug Pratt pp. 35–39;
and Andrew Vallely; p. 27, 29 (top).

HarperCollins books may be purchased for educational, business, or sales promotional use. For informa-
tion please write: Special Markets Department, HarperCollins Publishers Inc., 10 East 53rd Street, New
York, NY 10022.
First HarperResource paperback edition published 2003

Library of Congress Cataloging-in-Publication Data has been applied for.
ISBN 0-06-053336-6 (pbk.)
03 04 05 06 PE 10 9 8 7 6 5 4 3 2 1

Contents

HOW TO ATTRACT BIRDS

IDENTIFYING BACKYARD BIRDS

HOW TO ATTRACT BIRDS

by
SCOTT EDWARDS

here are four fundamental attractions for birds: food, water, shelter, and a place to raise their young, all of which are easily provided in backyards.

Food is the most basic and obvious bird attraction, and more birds are attracted to black-oil sunflower seeds ("oilers" to bird-feeding veterans) than to any other seed. The black-oil sunflower seeds are smaller compared to the more familiar large striped varieties. Other attractive seeds are thistle seeds, striped sunflower seeds, split peanuts, peanuts in the shell, white proso millet, and various nuts.

It is important to note that not everything labeled "birdseed" is eaten by birds. Many birdseed mixes contain filler products, seeds that add only weight and actually detract from the mix's attractiveness. Grains like milo, oats, wheat, rice, and canary seed, as well as the ambiguous "mixed grain products," are best avoided. Table scraps are not recommended for birds either. Bread crumbs, crackers, and similar foods are just empty calories that offer very little nutrition.

When most people think of bird-feeding, they think first of offering seed. However, only a

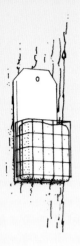

minority of the birds that surround us are seed-crushers. Many additional birds can be attracted to your feeding station if you offer suet, fruit, mealworms, or nectar.

Suet is the fat that surrounds beef kidneys. It will attract woodpeckers, chickadees, titmice, nuthatches, and brown creepers. It is also occasionally eaten by catbirds, mockingbirds, orioles, and pine warblers, among others. Suet is very dense and should not be confused with fat trimmings from other beef parts. Plain fat is not as beneficial, has a much higher water content, and will freeze in cold weather.

Suet is not just for winter feeding. Most commercially available suets have been rendered, meaning that they have been boiled repeatedly to remove impurities and to prevent them from going rancid. There is even "summer suet" or suet doughs that are made to survive hot weather without melting.

Suet is best attached directly to the trunk of a large deciduous tree, at least initially. This is where the birds that feed on suet look for their food in the wild.

Fruit like oranges, grapes, and bananas attract orioles and tanagers. Bug-eating birds such

as bluebirds, wrens, and many others readily take mealworms. And, of course, no feeding station would be complete without the presence of nectar for hummingbirds.

The accepted formula for hummingbird nectar is four to five parts water to one part plain table sugar. I don't recommend the use of commercially prepared nectars or the use of coloring. Do not use any artificial sweeteners or honey. It is important to maintain a nectar feeder regularly. Nectar ferments rapidly and can be hazardous to hummingbirds if left out for more than a day or two. Nectar should be changed more often in hot weather.

How to dispense bird food, particularly seed, is an important choice to make. There are three basic designs for seed feeders; the tube feeder, usually made of polycarbonate and designed to hang from a tree or hook; the open platform feeder, which may or may not be covered; and the hopper feeder, basically a platform feeder with a Plexiglas center (the hopper) to hold and dispense seed.

Most tube feeders are designed to dispense black-oil sunflower seeds. Nearly all of the small seed-eaters that perch on tube feeders have such a strong preference for oilers that

using a mixture of seeds is often counter-productive. If you are presently filling your tube feeders with mixed seeds, you have probably witnessed the birds employing a technique called "bill sweeping." By sweeping their beaks from side to side, the birds remove everything but the oilers. And you get to fill your tubes more often.

Some tube feeders have very small ports designed to dispense thistle (technically known as niger) seed. These feeders primarily attract goldfinches.

All tube feeders are designed for small birds. The jays, cardinals, grosbeaks, grackles, and woodpeckers are too big to use them. This is good for the small seed-eaters, which are often bullied off feeders that will accommo-date larger birds. But if you can only have one feeder, you should consider a hopper feeder.

Hopper feeders are the most popular type, and a well-designed one will provide enough room to attract a large variety of birds. Both perching birds and ground feeders will visit a hopper feeder with a large landing area. The large seed capacity of the hopper feeder is another attractive feature for the people who have to fill them. Many hopper feeders will hold several pounds of birdseed and don't

have to be filled every day. Because of the variety of birds a hopper feeder can attract, it is an excellent place to use a high-quality mixture of seeds.

The platform or fly-through feeder attracts perhaps the widest variety of birds. The open design of these feeders allows birds to come and go from all directions. There is no dispensing mechanism to clog, so you are free to use virtually any food or combination of foods. Use peanuts in the shell if you want regular visits from jays, woodpeckers, and nutcrackers. These feeders are also ideal for serving fruit during the warmer months. I attach suet to my platform feeder to increase visits from woodpeckers, titmice chickadees, and nuthatches.

About four times a year it is a good idea to give your feeders a thorough cleaning. Feeders can get dirty, and wet seed can mold rapidly, making a feeding station unhealthy. Once a season I take down all my feeders over the course of a few days, hose them, soak them in a strong solution of white vinegar, and scrub them with a long-handled brush designed for feeder cleaning. I use vinegar, not bleach, because of the toxicity of chlorine and the fact that it can cloud tube feeders. Regular cleaning will help insure a healthy feeding station in your yard.

All birds must drink and bathe, so the inclusion of a birdbath with a dripper or mister will greatly enhance the attractiveness of your backyard habitat to birds, as can a recirculating pond. Drippers and misters are accessories that attach to your outside water source and provide fresh, moving water for birds. Most drippers utilize a low-flow system that constantly drips water into your water feature.

Misters spray the area around your water feature with a fine mist. They are especially effective if your water feature is surrounded by foliage. While some birds hesitate to immerse themselves, they may "leaf-bathe," an action that has them rubbing their feathers against wet leaves. Misters are also very attractive to hummingbirds, which love to fly around in the mist these accessories create.

Nest boxes are used by many birds that nest in cavities (tree hollows). Bluebirds, nuthatches, wrens, and woodpeckers are a few of the species that will accept your hospitality if you erect the appropriate nest box. Some lucky people are even able to attract screech-owls!

Nest boxes should be made of untreated, unpainted wood. Red cedar or white pine $3/4$ to 1 inch thick is preferable. Preservative,

paints, or stains are unnecessary and may actually be harmful. The exact dimensions of the box vary depending on which bird you are attempting to attract. This information is readily available at any good library or nature center. Nest boxes must be maintained regularly and cleaned of nesting debris after each brood fledges. Keep a logbook on the progress of the birds using your nest boxes, especially one with bluebirds in it. All nest inspections should stop approximately ten days after the eggs hatch, or the nestlings may fledge prematurely.

Habitat enhancement is really the key to attracting the most interesting birds to your backyard. Successfully attracting a wide variety and number of birds to your backyard entails more than just supplying feeders, seed, a pond, or nest boxes, however. I have dozens of differ-ent feeders at my station, but there is more bird activity per square foot in my two brush piles (conglomerations of limbs, branches, and old Christmas trees) than anywhere else in my yard.

Juncos, towhees, and native sparrows such as the white-throated nest and feed in the brush piles, and all the little songbirds seek cover there when a Cooper's or sharp-shinned hawk comes looking for an easy meal. If a brush pile is impractical, consider letting a small section of

your backyard go wild. Don't mow, don't prune, just let it grow and watch the birds show up!

Add fruit-bearing trees to your backyard habitat (mountain ash, hackberry, mulberry, and sassafras, for example) and you can attract waxwings, mockingbirds, warblers, catbirds, and bluebirds. Coniferous trees and shrubs such as juniper and holly are wonderful bird attractions and provide cover as well as food.

You can find assistance in improving your backyard habitat at your local nature center and at some of the better wild bird supply stores. Don't be discouraged if your first improvements don't get immediate results. Over time your backyard can become an oasis for birds.

Keep a good pair of binoculars on your windowsill next to this guide to identify the rarer birds your feeder attracts. Binoculars for birding should be 7 or 8 power, bright, sharp, and easy to hold. Stay away from cute gadgets like zooms, perma- or insta-focus, and strange-colored lenses. If you wear eyeglasses, you should be able to leave them on while using your binoculars. The wider your binoculars' field of vision (a salesperson can explain how this is measured) the easier they will be to use.

HOW TO LOOK AT A BIRD

The way birds feed and their adaptations for feeding are the most important points to recognize in identifying and understanding a bird. For the beginner, the color and pattern of an unknown bird can be so striking that important points of shape and behavior go unnoticed. But feeding adaptations, especially bill shape, best reveal a bird's role in nature — its truest identity.

Owls, hawks, doves, woodpeckers, and many other birds are easily recognized by shape and behavior. Songbirds are more confusing. If you don't immediately recognize a songbird as a sparrow, a wren, or a warbler, for example, look at its bill shape. Is it a seed-crusher or a bug-eater? Seed-crushers have strong, conical bills for cracking seeds. The shape of a bug-eater's bill varies with the way it catches bugs.

conical bill

Most bug-eaters have slender, straight bills used to probe in trees, brush, ground litter, and rock crevices. A few have curved bills for specialized probing. And some, the flycatcher group, have broad-based, flat bills. Flycatchers catch bugs in midair, and their broad bills improve their chances of success.

straight bill

curved bill

flycatching bill

If bill shape can't be seen, a bird's feeding behavior is often just as revealing. Sparrows

14

don't flit among the branches of a tree searching for bugs, and warblers won't be seen on the ground picking at seeds.

Knowing its bill shape or feeding behavior reduces the possible identities of an unknown bird. Plumage marks can then be used to identify all the backyard species.

Most names used to describe parts of a bird are predictable — back, crown, throat, etc. Three names that might not be immediately understood are rump, undertail coverts, and wing bars. The rump is at the base of the tail, topside; undertail coverts cover the base of the tail, bottomside. Wing bars are formed by the contrasting tips (often white) of the feathers that help cover the wing when it is folded.

Underside of tail showing tail spots and undertail coverts.

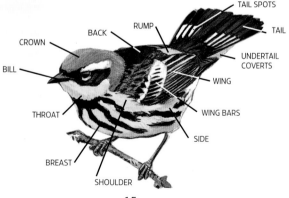

TAIL SPOTS

RUMP

BACK

TAIL

CROWN

BILL

UNDERTAIL COVERTS

WING

THROAT

WING BARS

SIDE

BREAST

SHOULDER

HOW TO READ THE MAPS

Range maps provide a simplified picture of a species' distribution. They indicate the birds that can be expected in any local region. Birds are not evenly distributed over their ranges. They require suitable habitat (no seeds, no sparrows) and are typically scarcest at their range limits. Some birds are numerous but not commonly seen because they are secretive.

Weather and food availability affect bird distribution in winter. Some birds regularly retreat south to escape winter weather. Others leave their northern ranges only occasionally. Some whose resident population slowly creeps northward in mild winters may perish if their newly occupied range is hit by a hard winter.

MAP KEY

SUMMER OR
NESTING

WINTER

ALL YEAR

MIGRATION
(spring & fall)

HOW THE BIRDS ARE ORGANIZED

OWLS AND NIGHTHAWK

EASTERN SCREECH-OWL

COMMON NIGHTHAWK

BARN OWL

The great horned owl might be heard from backyards. It gives a deep *hoo, hoo-hoo, hoo, hoo* or similar five- or six-note call.

Although seldom seen because they hunt in the evenings and at night, some owls are surprisingly common near houses and farms. **Eastern screech-owls** are often found in suburban woodlots or parks, where their calls — a long mournful whinny or a long low trill — can be heard. They are the only small owl in the East with ear tufts, or "horns." Sometimes the ear tufts are held flat, however, and are not visible. Screech-owls can be gray, brown, or a rusty red.

Barn owls are still numerous in the Southeast, but the northern population is seriously declining with loss of habitat and the great number of road kills. The **barn owl** is often recognized by its heart-shaped face. Its pale body and long legs are also good marks. Barn owls screech, and screech-owls give a whistling tone, proving that bird names are often misleading.

Nighthawks (another misleading name; they are not hawks) sweep through the skies feeding like swifts or swallows. They are locally common over woodlands and some towns and cities at dusk and dawn, but have declined markedly in the East in the last 25 years. Note the **nighthawk's** white wing patch and listen for its nasal *peent* flight call.

18

Eastern Screech-owl

young

gray form

red form

Common
Nighthawk

Barn Owl

VULTURES

TURKEY VULTURE

BLACK VULTURE

Vultures typically
soar on thermals and
updrafts. Because
black vultures have
shorter wings, they
don't soar as
buoyantly as turkey
vultures. Black
vultures have to flap
a bit more and might
stay grounded on a
day that a turkey
vulture could soar.

Large black birds with unfeathered heads seen tugging at a piece of road kill are easily recognized as vultures – the "buzzards" of the old West. Adult **turkey vultures** are the ones with red heads. Young turkey vultures are dark-headed, however, and can be mistaken for black vultures.

Dark-headed birds are best identified by shape, especially tail length. The **black vulture** is more compact and has a short tail that barely extends beyond the folded wing of a standing bird. Turkey vultures, young and old, are rangier birds with a longer tail.

When not feeding, vultures are usually seen soaring high overhead in search of carrion. Even at a great distance, they can often be recognized by their flight style and the contrasting pattern of pale and dark on their underwing. Only the outer wing feathers of the black vulture's wing are pale. Turkey vultures often tip a bit from side to side as they soar and usually hold their wings above horizontal in a shallow V. Black vultures soar on flat wings and often give a series of quick, shallow flaps.

Black vultures are less common than turkey vultures but are slowly expanding their range in the Northeast.

Turkey Vulture

black vulture

turkey vulture

black vulture

Black Vulture

HAWKS

KESTREL

RED-TAILED HAWK

The local breeding population of peregrine falcons in the East was largely lost to pesticide sprays in the mid-1900s.

Peregrines have been reintroduced in many eastern cities. They roost and nest on bridges and high buildings. Pigeons are their preferred meal.

The kestrel and red-tailed hawk are not likely to be seen in backyards, but they are common along roads and in parks. The red-tailed hawk is often seen soaring. A Kestrel hunts from a perch, typically a wire or pole overlooking a vacant lot or other open area. It will often return to the same perch daily if it is successful in capturing the mice, large insects, or small birds that are its prey. Kestrels often hover over suspected prey.

The **kestrel** is identified by its size, only 10 to 12 inches long, and two black face streaks contrasting with white cheeks and throat. Males are smaller than females, and the blue on the male's wings contrasts with the red on its back and tail. There is no such contrast in the upperparts of the female, which are an even red with heavy dark barring.

The red-tailed hawk seen soaring over your backyard is not likely to harass birds at your feeder like the hawks on the following pages do. Nearly all adult eastern **red-tailed hawks** have a red tail (pink from below) and dark streaks on the belly that often form a band. Young birds have brownish tails with many narrow dark bands. The dark bars along the leading edge of the underwing are good marks for identifying soaring birds.

young

Kestrel

♀

♂

eastern

western

Red-tailed Hawk

eastern

young

COOPER'S HAWK

SHARP-SHINNED HAWK

Young hawks of some larger species (buteos) may be confused with a young Cooper's, but they don't attack at backyard feeders as a Cooper's does. And Cooper's hawk seldom sits openly on roadside perches as buteos do.

ooper's and sharp-shinned hawks are the birds of prey known for attacking songbirds at backyard bird feeders and sometimes colliding with picture windows. They seldom perch openly or soar overhead like the hawks described on the previous pages. Instead, they typically lurk in foliage until prey appears and then, with a sprinter's explosive burst, ambush the unsuspecting dinner.

Except in size, the two species are nearly identical. Both **Cooper's** and the **sharp-shinned** have long tails with distinctive broad dark and pale bands. Adults are blue-gray above with rusty barring below. Young birds are brown above and have brown streaking on their underparts.

Size differences between Cooper's and the sharp-shinned are sometimes hard to judge. A small male sharpie (about 12 inches long) can be distinguished from a large female Cooper's (about 18 inches), but most individuals are somewhere in between.

Small differences in their tails are the best marks separating the two species but are very difficult to see. The tip of a Cooper's tail is round and banded white. The sharpie's tail has squarer corners and a narrow gray terminal band.

24

Typical variations in
sharp-shinned hawk's tail

young
sharp-shinned

Cooper's

young

young Cooper's

sharp-shinned

young

adults shown in typical
flight; young birds soaring

Cooper's Hawk

young

**Sharp-shinned
Hawk**

young

SWALLOWS

TREE SWALLOW

PURPLE MARTIN

BARN SWALLOW

Two other swallows are brown above and white below like young tree swallows. The bank swallow has a brown breast band; the rough-winged, a dirty-brown throat and upper breast.

Swallows are sleek and speedy aerialists that spend most of their day capturing bugs in flight. Because flying insects abound near water, swallows often fly over water. When not feeding, they can be seen together, side by side, on a wire by the dozens. Tree swallows nest in boxes; martins use communal nest boxes. Barn swallows commonly make cup-shaped mud nests under eaves.

It isn't easy to get a good look at a flying swallow, but most can be identified at a glance if you know what to look for. The **tree swallow** is the only eastern swallow that is white below and glossy blue-green above. Young birds are brown above. Note that the tree swallow doesn't have a "swallowtail."

The **barn swallow** is the swallow with the forked tail shape that has become a graphic symbol of speed and grace. The upperparts are a deep blue on all birds, but the orange-buff underparts can be paler on young birds. Also, the tail streamers of young birds are often shorter than the adults.

The **purple martin** is our largest swallow, and the only species in which the sexes differ strongly. The male is an even blue-black. Females are duller above and gray below with a gray collar.

Tree Swallow

Purple Martin

young

♂

♀

Barn Swallow

SWIFT AND HUMMINGBIRD

CHIMNEY SWIFT

RUBY-THROATED HUMMINGBIRD

Hummingbird feeders in the South are attracting increasing numbers of vagrant western and Mexican hummers in fall and over the winter.

Chimney swifts once roosted in hollow trees in the original eastern forest. Now they primarily use chimneys.

L ike the swallows shown on the previous pages, swifts collect insects in flight. Unlike swallows, they are never seen resting on a wire or branch. Except when roosting at night or sitting out bad weather, swifts are airborne.

The only eastern swift, the **chimney swift,** is a dark bird with a pale throat that flies rapidly and erratically. The flight style itself is the best mark distinguishing it from swallows. Rapid, shallow wing beats create a unique twinkling effect that, once seen, is easily noted. The swift can seem to flap its wings alternately. Swallows fly more gracefully.

The **ruby-throated hummingbird** is the only hummer that occurs throughout the East. It is the male that has the ruby throat, which most often appears flat black. Only when light is reflected at a favorable angle can the flash of ruby red be seen. Female hummers lack the male's brilliant throat feathers, although some may sport a few dots of red. Tail shapes of male and female ruby-throats are also distinctively different.

Hummingbirds are usually seen singly or in small numbers in spring, but larger numbers may congregate at a backyard feeder in late summer or early fall.

Chimney Swift

Ruby-throated
Hummingbird

♂

♀

GAMEBIRDS

BOBWHITE

RING-NECKED PHEASANT

Wild turkeys were once numerous in open woodlands of the South and East, then were hunted to scarcity in most areas. Now they are managed as a gamebird in all 48 adjacent states.

Gamebirds have learned to be very cautious and to stay hidden to protect themselves. They are prey to many wild animals, as well as humans. Only a few gamebirds are found on cultivated land or in areas near people.

The eastern gamebirds that live closest to humans are the bobwhite and the ring-necked pheasant. Bobwhites are common in fields and hedgerows and will even venture into rural backyards. Pheasants are common in farmlands, but local populations regularly plummet and rebound.

Bobwhites are a species of quail. They live in coveys (small flocks) most of the time. When nesting and raising young, they are paired. Identifying a **bobwhite** is usually just a matter of recognizing its call, a whistled *bob-white!* Males are reddish brown with a white throat and eyebrow. Females are duller and have a buff throat and eyebrow.

Pheasants were introduced from Asia and have a number of color variations. Some males have green bodies; others have white wings; some lack the neck ring. All males have a red eye patch. The most common form is illustrated. Both sexes have distinctive long pointed tails.

30

Bobwhite

♀ ♂

Ring-necked
Pheasant

♀ ♂

DOVES

COMMON GROUND-DOVE

MOURNING DOVE

ROCK DOVE

Eurasian collared-doves are now common in some southern cities. They have a black collar like a ringed turtle-dove (a cage bird), but give a *coo-coo-coo* instead of the turtle-dove's bubbling call.

Doves (or pigeons — there is no difference) can be depended on to show up at backyard feeders. They have very short legs and walk on the ground like game-birds rather than hopping along like most birds. As they walk, they bob their heads back and forth in a characteristic fashion.

The **common ground-dove** was once common along the Gulf of Mexico. Large numbers remain only in Florida. Smaller than the mourning or rock dove, it has a scaled breast and flashes rusty red in its wings when it flies.

Mourning doves and rock doves are widespread and abundant. **Mourning doves** are the ones with long pointed tails. Doves are a popular symbol for peace, but at a feeder, mourning doves can be quite aggressive among themselves. A mournful call, *woo-oó-oo, oo, oo, oo,* is given in spring and summer by unmated males.

Rock dove is the formal name for the well-known pigeon of cities and farms. It originally nested on cliffs. Pigeons have colonized most of the world in the company of man. The many color variations seen are the result of interbreeding with exotic domesticated strains. The ancestral form is shown in the foreground.

32

Common Ground-dove

♂ ♀

Mourning Dove

Rock Dove

WOODPECKERS

T he most common woodpecker in eastern backyards is the downy. It is also the smallest, just 7 inches long. The hairy woodpecker has virtually the identical plumage pattern but is 2 inches larger. It is a frequent visitor to suet feeders.

DOWNY WOODPECKER

HAIRY WOODPECKER

The size difference is easy to recognize when the two species are seen side by side, but can be hard to judge when the birds are seen separately. The best mark is the bill length. The **hairy woodpecker** has a much larger bill — nearly as long as its head. The **downy woodpecker's** bill extends only about half its head length.

The pileated woodpecker is sometimes seen in mature trees in parks or woodlots. It is a large, mostly black bird the size of a crow, with a pointed, flaming red crest and white wing patches.

Males of both species have a bright red patch on the back of their crowns that is lacking in females. Young birds (both sexes) also show a patch of red on their heads, but the color is more diffuse and is located on the center or forepart of the crown rather than on the rear.

There is a very small plumage difference that can be noted on birds at close range. The white outer tail feathers on the hairy woodpecker are unmarked, while those on the downy woodpecker have two or more black bars.

young

hairy

Downy
Woodpecker

♀

♂

Hairy
Woodpecker

♀

♂

WOODPECKERS

RED-BELLIED WOODPECKER

YELLOW-SHAFTED FLICKER

The red-bellied woodpecker is some-times mistakenly called a red-headed woodpecker.

There is a red-headed woodpecker, and it was once common. The adult has a com-pletely red head and neck. It has become scarce as a result of competition for nest holes with starlings.

S everal different woodpeckers show up regularly in backyards, particularly at suet feeders. The red-bellied woodpecker on these pages and the hairy and downy woodpeckers on the previous pages are the most commonly seen.

The yellow-shafted flicker (a woodpecker) is much rarer at suet feeders. It is usually seen on the ground in parks or other open short-grass areas feeding on ants, its favorite meal. Flickers also gather insects from trees like other woodpeckers, but because they often feed on the ground, they are sometimes not recognized as woodpeckers.

The typical view of a **yellow-shafted flicker** is of a white-rumped bird rising in flight from the ground and flying directly away, flashing yellow in the underwing. Seen closer, the flicker has strikingly patterned plumage. The male has a black mustache mark lacking in females.

Red-bellied woodpeckers do have a red belly, but it is a small pale red blush that isn't a good field mark. The black-and-white barred back, or "ladder-back," is a better mark. The red patch on the nape and hind neck of the female continues over the crown and forehead on the male.

36

red-headed woodpecker

♂

♀

**Red-bellied
Woodpecker**

**Yellow-shafted
Flicker**

♂

♀

NUTHATCHES AND CREEPER

WHITE-BREASTED NUTHATCH

RED-BREASTED NUTHATCH

BROWN CREEPER

The black-and-white warbler (p. 68) behaves a lot like a nuthatch, picking insects from limbs and trunks of trees.

Not all birds seen climbing a tree trunk are woodpeckers. Nuthatches and the brown creeper also make a living on the insects and larvae hidden in a tree's bark. Nuthatches are the only tree-climbers so agile that they can creep down a tree. Presumably they find morsels that upward-climbers miss. They also forage for insects at the tips of small branches and take seeds from pine cones.

The **white-breasted nuthatch** is the most common nuthatch at most feeders. It is dark above and white below with an inconspicuous wash of rusty red on its flanks. Females are the same as males, except some are noticeably grayer on the crown.

Red-breasted nuthatches prefer conifers and are common only in the northern portion of the eastern US. They are smaller and even bolder than the white-breasted. Note the rusty red underparts and black eyestripe. Females are duller than males.

The **brown creeper** is often overlooked. It can appear on the trunk of any tree, especially mature ones, and blends into the background of bark. It spirals up a tree trunk and is often first noticed flying from one tree to the base of another.

White-breasted
Nuthatch

♀

Red-
breasted
Nuthatch

♂

Brown Creeper

WAXWING AND KINGBIRD

EASTERN KINGBIRD

CEDAR WAXWING

In coastal Florida, especially the Keys, the gray kingbird can often be seen perched on utility wires. As its name suggests, it is grayer above than the eastern kingbird. It also lacks the white tip to its notched tail and has a narrow black mask.

Waxwings wander in flocks of up to a hundred birds or so except when nesting. They keep in close contact, giving a pleasing high-pitched, lisping call. A flock of these sleek birds will often sit awhile in the top of a tall tree before flying down to feed on fruit or berries. They also catch insects, flycatcher fashion, in summer.

The small dots of red on the wings are the source of the waxwing's name. They suggest the wax once used for sealing documents. The crest, narrow dark mask, and yellow tail tip are the easiest marks for identifying the **cedar waxwing.** It is the only eastern bird with a yellow-tipped tail, and the **eastern kingbird** is the only one with a white-tipped tail.

The eastern kingbird is a flycatcher like the eastern phoebe and great crested flycatcher shown on the next pages. All wait patiently for an insect to pass their perch. After catching it on the wing, the flycatcher often returns to the same perch to repeat the process.

The kingbird is particularly conspicuous, preferring a high perch in an open area from which to watch for flying insects. Its noisy, aggressive behavior also draws attention. Other birds or people that come too near a nest are subject to attack.

Eastern Kingbird

Cedar Waxwing

young

EASTERN PHOEBE

**GREAT CRESTED
FLYCATCHER**

**Most often confused
with the phoebe
are the eastern
wood-pewee and
the empidonax
flycatchers.**

**The empidonax are a
closely related group
of flycatchers that
have white wing
bars and eye rings.
Pewees have wing
bars but no eye rings.**

ne of the most familiar flycatchers,
the eastern phoebe has adapted
well to civilization and frequently nests under
eaves or bridges, or on any flat surface pro-
tected by an overhang. Barns are especially
popular nest sites because of the abundance
of flying insects. Like many other songbirds,
phoebes often return each spring to the
same nest site.

There are other small flycatchers (see
sidebar) resembling a phoebe — dark above,
pale below — but only the **eastern phoebe**
pumps its tail downward. The name comes
from its call, a forceful *fee-bee,* alternately rising and falling in pitch and given repeatedly.

The great crested flycatcher is common in
forests and orchards and ventures to the
shade trees of residential areas. Like the
eastern kingbird shown on the previous page,
it can be noisy and aggressive. The **great
crested flycatcher's** yellow belly is a good
mark, but the best mark is often the rusty red
flash in the wings and tail of the bird as it flies.

All flycatchers are migrants, heading south
when summer ends. Phoebes are the hardiest,
the only flycatcher wintering in the eastern
US, except for a few great crested flycatchers
that remain in South Florida.

Eastern Phoebe

young

Great Crested
Flycatcher

BROWN THRASHER

HOUSE WREN

CAROLINA WREN

Winter wrens are scarce but could show up in a backyard brush pile. They are a smaller version of the house wren with an even stubbier tail and a buff eyebrow.

The thrashers and wrens have curved bills that they use to probe for bugs. Thrashers use their bills to rake the soil and leaf litter under shrubs and bushes for insects. Because they are shy and often hidden, thrashers are frequently heard thrashing through the debris under a bush before they are seen. When surprised, they usually fly straight and low into a nearby bush.

The **brown thrasher** is sometimes confused with the wood thrush (p. 56). Both birds are rusty brown above and spotted below, but the brown thrasher has a curved bill and a longer tail. Also, its spots form streaks.

Wrens are not likely to be confused with other birds, even if their slightly curved bill is not noticed. No other small brown bird has similar fine barring on its wings and tail, and none cock their tail or scold so expressively. The **Carolina wren's** white eyebrow and buff underparts are the easiest marks separating it from the house wren. There is little to distinguish the mousy little **house wren** other than its wren shape and fine barring.

The Carolina and the house wrens are both common around houses. In the area above the dotted line on the map, the Carolina wren disappears after particularly hard winters.

44

Brown Thrasher

wood thrush
p. 56

House Wren

Carolina Wren

COMMON GRACKLE

AMERICAN CROW

FISH CROW

Boat-tailed grackles inhabit coastal marshes and Florida. Great-tailed grackles inhabit western Gulf states. Males of both species are half again as big as common grackles.

ost people with backyard feeders would consider grackles all too common. They feed in open areas and are opportunists that will eat grains, insects, or almost anything else they can subdue. The conversion of forest to open land throughout the East has allowed them to proliferate.

The **common grackle** has a longer tail than similar black birds seen near suburbs and farms. The tails of males in summer are distinctively wedge shaped, and in flight the central feathers are often depressed, creating a "keel" shape rather than a flat surface.

Adult male grackles have a purple or bronze sheen to their black plumage. Females show less sheen and only on the head, breast, and upper back. Young birds are a dull brown with brown, not yellow, eyes.

Crows and their larger relatives, ravens, are considered the most intelligent birds. Like grackles, they have benefitted from fields replacing forest. Scientists recognize two species in the East, the **fish crow** and the **American crow.** Fish crows are numerous in coastal marshes. They average a bit smaller than American crows, but the only reliable mark is their call, a two-noted nasal *eh-eh* rather than the familiar *caw.*

46

young
Common Grackle
♀
♂

American and
Fish Crows

BLUE JAY

MOCKINGBIRD

RED–WINGED BLACKBIRD

The loggerhead shrike can be found sometimes on roadside fences. The shrike is like a mocker but has a shorter bill, a black mask, and a different white wing patch.

A common and familiar bird, especially in the South, the mockingbird will perch conspicuously on a wire, limb, or often a TV antenna and serenade tirelessly throughout the year, even into the night. It is a famous mimic and will repeat grating, mechanical sounds as readily as the songs of other birds. The **mockingbird** is a slim gray bird with a long tail that it often holds erect. The white in its wings is a prominent mark when it flies.

Noisy and colorful, the **blue jay** is familiar to backyard birders. It dominates at a feeder and often fills its crop (a storage pouch in the throat) with sunflower seeds before flying off. It stores the seeds in the woods for winter or in case you forget to refill your feeder.

Red-winged blackbirds are widely known by the male's orange-red shoulder patches, although often only the yellowish lower border is visible when the bird is at rest. The female looks like a big streaked sparrow, sometimes with a bit of red blush on the face or shoulder. She is much scarcer around feeders than the male. Young birds look like females. The young male gradually acquires his adult plumage by fall of his second year.

48

Blue Jay

Mockingbird

mockingbird

loggerhead shrike

Red-winged
Blackbird

♂

♀

STARLING AND COWBIRD

STARLING

BROWN-HEADED COWBIRD

Another cowbird, the shiny cowbird from the Caribbean, is invading the East. It reached Florida in 1985 and is spreading throughout the state but is still rare.

Male shiny cowbirds are black with a violet gloss; females are similar to the brown-headed female.

The starling and cowbird are the villains among birds. Neither is native to the East, and both have raised havoc with native birds as their numbers have multiplied.

Originally introduced from Europe, the starling nests in cavities and has displaced native cavity nesters such as the purple martin (p. 26), the red-headed woodpecker and the eastern bluebird (p. 58).

The **starling's** plumage varies by season from spotted to glossy black. The birds have very short tails and long pointed bills. **The brown-headed cowbird's** best mark is its short conical bill. Males are black with a dark brown head; females, a dull gray-brown. Cowbirds are illustrated here rather than with the other conically billed birds because they are easily confused with blackbirds and starlings.

Cowbirds were originally birds of the Great Plains and were then known as "buffalo birds." They spread across the East when the original forest was felled. Cowbirds are nest parasites. They lay an egg in other birds' nests, and the host birds raise the cowbird chick, usually at the expense of their own young. Since mankind is responsible for the spread of the cowbird and the introduction of the starling, perhaps we are the villains.

fall

young

Starling

spring

molting young ♂
in fall

**Brown-headed
Cowbird**

♀

♂

ORIOLES

Adult male orioles are unmistakable, but females and young birds can be confusing. Female **orchard orioles** are olive green above and yellow to yellow-green below with two white wing bars. They lack the orange tones of the female Baltimore oriole and are noticeably smaller.

Young orchard orioles in their first summer and fall look very much like the female. The young males take two years to become adult, and the yearling male has a black chin and throat that distinguishes it from females and younger birds.

Female and young **Baltimore orioles** are particularly variable. Some females can show a lot of black on the head or throat (similar to the male) and have warm orange tones below. Other females, particularly young birds, can be yellowish and plain. Yearling males show orange and black splotches.

Female orioles can be confused with the female tanager shown on the next pages, as well as with each other. Note, however, that the female tanager lacks wing bars and has a distinctively shaped "swollen" bill.

Orioles often build their hanging, pendant-shaped nests in large shade trees.

ORCHARD ORIOLE

BALTIMORE ORIOLE

Orioles, meadow-larks, and blackbirds are all closely related, as can be seen by the bill shape in particular. All belong to a family known as icterids.

Orioles are fond of fruit and will feed on a halved orange or from a hummingbird-style nectar feeder.

young ♂

Orchard Oriole

♀

♂

Baltimore Oriole

♀

♂

young ♂

TANAGER AND MEADOWLARK

SCARLET TANAGER

EASTERN MEADOWLARK

There are two species of meadowlarks. The eastern meadowlark is the most common in the East, but western meadowlarks extend as far east as the Great Lakes.

Western meadowlarks look the same but have a different song, a bubbling, flute-like melody.

Scarlet tanagers are not common in residential areas, but they are regular spring migrants and summer visitors in shade trees. More aren't seen because they are relatively slow-moving birds that often stay hidden in the canopy of mature trees.

Scarlet tanagers are best located by their song and call. The song suggests a robin's whistled phrases but is distinctively hoarser. The call is also hoarse, a two-noted *chip-burr.*

By fall, males begin molting to a yellowish green plumage like the female's, but the wings and tail remain black. Patchy males can be seen before the birds begin fall migration.

From a perch on a rural fence post or wire, the **eastern meadowlark** often sings its familiar *see-you, see-yeer* song. It is almost as well known for its song as for its bright yellow breast with a black V. It flies with quail-like rapid strokes interrupted by short glides. The white outer tail feathers are often fanned when it glides.

Meadowlarks are seriously declining in the disappearing fields and meadows of the Northeast. They remain common only in their southern range. In fall and winter, they are often in flocks.

54

spring ♂

Scarlet Tanager

fall molting ♂

♀

Eastern Meadowlark

winter

summer

WOOD THRUSH AND ROBIN

WOOD THRUSH

ROBIN

The only spotted thrush to be seen in winter is the hermit thrush. It might be encountered in a wooded park, especially in the Southeast. It has a reddish tail (which it often pumps) contrasting with a browner back.

Both the wood thrush and the robin are backyard birds. The robin is seen in the open, sunny part of the yard, while the wood thrush prefers shadows and cover. Robins vastly outnumber wood thrushes.

There are several spotted thrushes in addition to the wood thrush that migrate to North America to nest. All are birds of the forest floor and all look much alike, gray-brown to reddish brown above and white below with breast spots. Wood thrushes are the only ones to adapt to backyards, but others might show up during migration.

The bold spotting is a good mark for the **wood thrush,** but the best mark is the contrast of the rusty head and back with the browner rump and tail.

One of the first birds every child learns to recognize is the **robin.** But how many people ever grow up to notice that female robins are distinctively duller above and paler orange below than males? Young birds have spotted breasts like the thrushes, and in fact, robins are thrushes.

The thrushes are accomplished singers. Their distinctive whistled flute-like notes are given in short phrases and carry well.

Wood Thrush

young

young

♂

Robin

STRAIGHT BILLS

BLUEBIRD AND CATBIRD

EASTERN BLUEBIRD

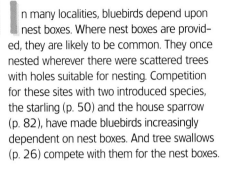

CATBIRD

Like robins, bluebirds are a member of the thrush family. They primarily catch prey on the ground like other thrushes, but bluebirds often sit on a fence or low wire to spot their prey.

In many localities, bluebirds depend upon nest boxes. Where nest boxes are provided, they are likely to be common. They once nested wherever there were scattered trees with holes suitable for nesting. Competition for these sites with two introduced species, the starling (p. 50) and the house sparrow (p. 82), have made bluebirds increasingly dependent on nest boxes. And tree swallows (p. 26) compete with them for the nest boxes.

The female **eastern bluebird** is much paler than the impressive male, with bright blue only in the wings and tail. The blue is palest in young birds, which also have spotting on their backs and breasts. Family groups are often seen together throughout the summer. They prefer open habitat with scattered trees. Orchards are a particular favorite.

The catbird is a skulker, much more common in the bushes and thickets of backyards and parks than many bird-watchers suspect. It is closely related to the mockingbird and sings a similar jumble of mimicked sounds and odd notes. Its name comes from a cat-like mewing that it often makes.

The only distinctive marks on the plain gray **catbird** are the rusty patch under the tail, which is hard to see, and the black cap.

58

young

♀

Eastern Bluebird

♂

Catbird

VIREOS

BLUE-HEADED VIREO

RED-EYED VIREO

WARBLING VIREO

Vireos are often confused with warblers, but a vireo's bill is heavier, more swollen, and vireos feed lethargically.

Although one of the most abundant birds in the East, the red-eyed vireo is not commonly seen. It is hidden in foliage high in trees, from forests to woodlands to backyards. Compared to most small birds, it moves slowly and deliberately as it picks insects from the foliage.

All the vireos forage much like the red-eyed, and all can often be heard singing as they feed. Each vireo states a phrase and then repeats it or a slight variation monotonously, with short pauses in between.

The **red-eyed vireo** runs several notes together, as a robin does, with an inflection up or down at the end of its phrase. The **warbling vireo** has a dozen or more clear notes in its rambling phrase. The **blue-headed** vireo gives a short phrase like the red-eyed, but it is richer, sweeter, usually given more slowly and with longer pauses.

Eye markings and wing bars are the best way to separate vireos visually. The blue-headed has spectacles; the warbling and red-eyed vireos have distinctive eyebrows. All can show pale yellow sides, but only the blue-headed vireo has wing bars. And don't look for red in the eye of the red-eyed; it's hard to see except in good light. The eye usually looks dark.

Blue-headed Vireo

Red-eyed Vireo

Warbling Vireo

yellow
extreme

WARBLERS

MYRTLE WARBLER

CHESTNUT-SIDED WARBLER

Two other warblers in the East have yellow rumps, the magnolia and the Cape May warblers.

The magnolia warbler is described on the next pages. The male Cape May warbler has a red patch around its eye. It is usually seen in ornamental spruce or pine.

Thirty-seven different kinds of warblers — each more beautiful than the other — nest in or migrate through eastern North America. Almost any of them might choose your backyard for a brief layover. The myrtle warbler is one of the most likely visitors; the chestnut-sided warbler is more likely to be seen in an overgrown pasture or a park.

To identify any warbler, begin by noting whether or not it shows yellow and whether or not it has wing bars. If you can get these two marks first and then note any other prominent features, you will have the best chance of success.

Both the **myrtle** and the **chestnut-sided warbler** show yellow and have wing bars. The chestnut-colored side stripe is an obvious mark for male chestnut-sided warblers. It can be absent on young birds seen in fall. Their best mark is the distinctive lime green upperparts and yellow wing bars.

The myrtle warbler has a yellow rump. There is also a distinctive patch of yellow on the side near the shoulder, although it is sometimes faint on young birds in fall. The myrtle is the most abundant eastern warbler in winter, when it feeds heavily on the myrtle berries from which it gets its name.

62

young

♀

spring ♂

Myrtle Warbler

Chestnut-sided Warbler

spring ♂

young

spring ♀

WARBLERS

BLACK-THROATED
GREEN WARBLER

**BLACK-THROATED
GREEN WARBLER**

**MAGNOLIA
WARBLER**

Few warblers
actually warble.
Their songs tend to
be high-pitched
notes and trills.
A warbling song is
most likely given
by a vireo or finch.

Like the warblers shown on the previous pages, the black-throated green and the magnolia warbler show yellow and have distinctive wing bars. Both are numerous and could well appear in the trees or bushes of your backyard during migration. They are even more likely to be seen in a woodland park.

These warblers are also good examples of the typical variations in a warbler's plumage. In most warblers, the boldness of their colors varies with sex, season, age, or all three, but the pattern remains similar. There are a few species, however, in which male and female or spring and fall birds look distinctly different.

Black-throated green warblers don't always have a black throat. The throat is a good mark in adult males and most females, but young birds in fall have white throats. The best mark is the yellow face bordered on the crown and neck with olive green.

Magnolia warblers retain the large band of white in their tail in all plumages. When the tail is half spread, the white becomes an easy mark. The black mask and breast streaks are obvious on spring birds, but in fall, the black mask is gone and the black breast streaks and throat band are replaced by vague grayish markings in many birds.

Black-throated Green Warbler

♀

♂

young

♀

young

spring ♂

Magnolia Warbler

WARBLERS

YELLOW WARBLER

COMMON YELLOWTHROAT

Only the prothonotary and the blue-winged warbler are as bright yellow as the yellow warbler.

Prothonotaries are so bright that the males almost glow. The wings and tail, however, are blue-gray. The blue-winged warbler has white wing bars and a black eyeline.

The yellowthroat and yellow warbler show yellow but do not have wing bars, as the four warblers shown on the previous pages do. The yellow warbler can have narrow yellow wing bars, but they are generally lost in the overall yellow of the bird.

The male **common yellowthroat** is recognized by its black mask. Females and young birds are more difficult to identify. First, note the yellow and the lack of wing bars. There is yellow on the throat and under the rump, but the belly is brownish gray. The absence of yellow on the belly is the most distinctive mark. The brown cheek is also a useful mark. Yellow extends onto the cheek of most warblers with yellow underparts.

Both of these warblers are common. They forage in shrubs and thickets, and a few are likely to visit backyard bushes or the lower branches of shade trees. If your backyard borders a wetland, you are especially likely to see these birds regularly.

Most **yellow warblers** are bright yellow, and males have red breast streaks. Young birds can be confusing. Look for the beady dark eye and the yellow edges on their wing feathers, which give the wings a striped effect. In flight, the yellow tail spots are visible.

♀ and young

♂

Yellow Warbler

olive extreme
young

Common Yellowthroat

young ♂

♂

♀

WARBLERS

BLACK-AND-WHITE WARBLER

AMERICAN REDSTART

The male blackpoll warbler can be confused with the black-and-white, but it is a late spring migrant and is usually in the canopy, hidden by foliage.

Male blackpoll warblers have a solid black cap and less dramatic striping.

Black-and-white warblers are one of the earliest spring migrants. They are relatively easy to see because they arrive when trees are still bare. Like the nuthatches (p. 38), they scour the trunks and large limbs of trees for insects and larvae.

There is no yellow on the **black-and-white warbler,** and it has white wing bars. The black and white stripes on its head and body distinguish it from all other warblers. Note the black throat that distinguishes the male in spring. The male's throat is white in fall, but the patch around the eye remains black. It is grayish or lacking in females.

Redstarts are warblers, and the American redstart is one of the most beautiful. Latin America got it right when they named it *candelita,* or "little torch."

The salmon color on the male **American redstart** is replaced by yellow on the female. The patches in the wings are not wing bars. Wing bars are nearer the shoulder of a bird, not on the flight feathers themselves. When feeding in a shrub or tree, the American redstart is very active, flashing the bright colors in its wings and tail. It is often seen chasing flying bugs in short, wild flights.

Black-and-white Warbler

♀

spring ♂

♀

American Redstart

♂

CHICKADEES AND TITMOUSE

TUFTED TITMOUSE

CAROLINA CHICKADEE

BLACK-CAPPED CHICKADEE

The rise that the artist, Larry McQueen, shows on the hind neck of the black-capped may look unusual but is often displayed. Check for it on your chickadees.

Some of the boldest and also most welcome birds at backyard feeders are the chickadees and the tufted titmouse. The birds are closely related and have similar habits. During the summer, they feed mostly on insects and visit feeders infrequently. In winter, they regularly attend backyard feeders to eat seeds, nuts, and suet.

A perky crest and buff flanks distinguish the **tufted titmouse.**

Whether you see the **Carolina chickadee** or the **black-capped chickadee** depends upon where your backyard is. There is only a narrow band where the ranges of the two birds overlap, and in that band there are some hybrids.

The chickadees can be separated by a subtle but noticeable plumage mark. Check the wings. The Carolina chickadee can show some white or pale streaking on the folded wing, but the black-capped has distinct white in the folded wing and forming a bar on the shoulder. Black-caps have a four-syllable song, *fee-bee, fee-bay.* Carolinas give two or three notes, *fee-bee* or *fee-bee-ee.* The call of both birds is the same: a clear, scolding *chick-a-dee-dee-dee,* given slightly faster and higher-pitched by the Carolina chickadee.

70

Tufted Titmouse

Carolina Chickadee

Black-capped Chickadee

KINGLETS AND GNATCATCHER

RUBY-CROWNED KINGLET

GOLDEN-CROWNED KINGLET

BLUE-GRAY GNATCATCHER

The tiny kinglets and gnatcatchers are closely related in spite of their different shapes. Kinglets nest in northern conifers and are usually seen in eastern parks in migration and winter. They occasionally visit backyard shrubs and trees but not feeders. The ruby-crowned kinglet takes a few seeds in winter, but all kinglets manage to find hidden larvae and insect matter even in cold and snowy weather.

The color of its crown and the white eyebrow are good marks for the **golden-crowned kinglet. Ruby-crowned kinglets** are more nondescript; only the male shows red, and it is usually concealed. The tiny bill, plump body, and short tail give the ruby-crowned a different look from the warblers it might be confused with. The clinching marks are a white eye-ring broken at the top and a white wing bar bordered below by a dark patch — the kinglet patch.

The **blue-gray gnatcatcher** is the only tiny, slim bird with a long tail likely to be seen in eastern backyards. It is very fidgety, often cocking its tail expressively and flashing the white underside. Both sexes have a white eye-ring; males have a narrow black eyebrow and a blue-gray crown. Gnatcatchers feed on bugs, picking them from leaves and from the air, often in the crown of a shade tree.

72

Ruby-crowned Kinglet

Golden-crowned Kinglet

Blue-gray Gnatcatcher

summer ♂

CARDINAL AND TOWHEE

CARDINAL

EASTERN TOWHEE

Widely known as the rufous-sided towhee, the eastern towhee got its new name in 1995 when it was determined to be a separate species from similar birds in the West.

ften the first to arrive at a backyard feeder in the morning and the last to stop by for a snack before dark, cardinals are the main reason many people have backyard feeders. The cardinal's range has steadily expanded northward because of the availability of sunflower seeds at feeders, allowing them to overwinter.

Even the brownish female **cardinal** is easily recognized by its crest, the red in its wings and tail, and its heavy conical bill. Young birds look like females but have dull bills instead of the bright orange-red bills of females.

The eastern towhee is declining at a faster rate than any other bird in the East. Like the brown thrasher (p. 44) and wood thrush (p. 56), it feeds in ground litter and is almost always hidden in shadows and shrubs. Parks and roadsides can provide good habitat, and so can a brushy backyard area.

The rusty-colored sides are good marks for adult **eastern towhees.** Males have black hoods and backs; females, brown. Long black tails with white in the corners are prominent marks for both the adults and the streaked, brown young birds. Their song, a distinctive *drink-your-tea,* or their namesake *tow-hee* call is often the best clue to the bird's presence.

74

Cardinal

Eastern Towhee

♀

♂

♀

young

GROSBEAKS

Big finches with very heavy bills, the grosbeaks are special visitors to back-yard feeders. Rose-breasted grosbeaks usually visit only in spring and are often seen in pairs. Evening grosbeaks gather in wandering flocks and show up at feeders in winter.

Rose-breasted grosbeaks eat insects as much as seeds in summer, so they are seldom regular visitors to a sunflower seed station. In spring, adult male **rose-breasted grosbeaks** are impressively beautiful and easy to identify. In fall, they look a lot like females but keep their black wings and tail and a rose blush on their breasts.

The female has striped underparts like many smaller finches. The large bill and distinct head stripes are her best marks. Young birds in fall resemble the female; young males have buff breasts. Males of all ages have red underwings; females, yellow.

The male **evening grosbeak** wears the same color plumage all year. The large white wing patches, stubby tail, and yellow forehead and eyebrows are all easily seen marks. Females are much grayer and have smaller white wing patches. Evening grosbeaks are attracted by road salt as well as sunflower seeds. They are relatively tame birds that move deliberately.

ROSE-BREASTED GROSBEAK

EVENING GROSBEAK

Pine grosbeaks are occasional winter visitors from the north to as far south as Pennsylvania and New Jersey. They flock like evening grosbeaks, but the male is red with white wing bars; the female, gray with an olive head and rump.

♀ ♂ young fall ♂

Rose-breasted
Grosbeak

Evening Grosbeak

♂

♀

FINCHES AND BUNTING

AMERICAN GOLDFINCH

PINE SISKIN

INDIGO BUNTING

Blue grosbeaks are much like indigo buntings. The blue grosbeak is an inch or two larger and has a heavier bill and rusty-brown wing bars.

➤

oldfinches are easily attracted to back-yards by thistle seed feeders. Indigo buntings are summer visitors and are much rarer in backyards, preferring the scrubby growth of roadsides and fencerows. Pine siskins visit in winter, irregularly.

Although the male **American goldfinch** in summer plumage is easily recognized, female and fall birds are a dull, unstreaked olive brown above. Their white undertails are good marks. Males in winter resemble females but retain their black wings and tail and a small, bright yellow shoulder patch.

Pine siskins have a sharply pointed bill for a finch — a small mark, but a good one, sepa-rating them from other brown striped finches. The yellow, mostly in the wings, is not obvious.

Only the male **indigo bunting** in spring and summer is an iridescent indigo blue, and in shadow it often looks black. The female and young are dull brown with vague streaking on their breasts. Some can show a flash of blue in their wings and tail or a pale blue wash on the rump and shoulder. Brown birds with patches of bright blue plumage are males, either adults in fall, molting to their brown winter plumage, or yearlings in spring that are still acquiring the full breeding plumage.

American Goldfinch

winter

summer ♂

summer ♀

Pine Siskin

American goldfinch

pine siskin

yearling ♂

spring ♂

fall ♂

Indigo Bunting

♀

RED FINCHES

HOUSE FINCH

PURPLE FINCH

An Arctic finch, the common redpoll, sometimes invades the northern states in winter in large flocks. It resembles a small female house finch but has a well-defined patch of red on the forehead and some black around the bill.

Both house and purple finches are seen in backyards, often in the same backyard. It wasn't always so. House finches are a western species introduced in Long Island, New York, in the 1940s. They have proliferated, partly at the expense of the purple finch.

Males of both species have a splash of red that varies considerably among individuals. Separating the two species requires care. The females are plain, brown-striped birds that require even more care in identification.

House finches are a little slimmer than **purple finches** and have smaller heads and bills. Side by side the difference is perceptible. The best mark for male house finch is the distinct brown streaking on its sides and belly. Purple finches have blurry, reddish side streaks at most. The red on the male house finch's head is concentrated on the forehead and eyebrows. On the purple finch, the red extends onto the crown, nape, and back and tends to be more wine-colored.

The contrast of the broad white eyebrow and whisker stripe on the female purple finch is her best mark. The face of the female house finch is much plainer; her breast streaks are a bit finer and extend all the way under her less deeply notched tail.

House Finch

♀

♂

Purple Finch

♂

♀

JUNCO AND SPARROW

DARK-EYED JUNCO

HOUSE SPARROW

Snow bird is one of the popular and very appropriate names for the junco. When the weather turns cold and snow is forecast, the juncos return. The house sparrow has also inspired many popular names, including English sparrow and feathered rat.

Eastern juncos look different from western ones. Scientists have often reversed themselves on whether juncos in the East are a separate species (the slate-colored junco) or a race of the dark-eyed junco. Currently they are considered a race.

Call them what you will, **juncos** in the East are easy to identify. The white outer tail feathers and white belly contrast conspicuously with the slate gray back and hood. Also note the pale bill. Females are duller, browner, and can show contrast between the hood and the back.

House sparrows were introduced to New York from Europe in 1851. After years of expanding their range and numbers, they now inhabit neighborhoods and farms (but not wild areas) throughout the United States. They are beginning to decline, although perhaps not at your feeder. Male **house sparrows** have a black bib and chestnut head markings. The female is best identified by the combination of plain underparts, pale eyebrow, and pale bill.

Dark-eyed
Junco

♀

♂

fall ♂

House
Sparrow

♀

♂

CROWNED SPARROWS

WHITE-THROATED SPARROW

WHITE-CROWNED SPARROW

Prominent black and white crown stripes distinguish adult white-throated and white-crowned sparrows. Both are regularly seen on the ground at feeders in backyards, usually in winter or during migration. White-throated sparrows are more common in most areas but a bit more secretive than white-crowneds and a little more reluctant to show themselves at a feeder.

White-throated and white-crowned sparrows are both a little larger than most sparrows. The best mark for the **white-crowned sparrow** (after the black-and-white crown of the adult) is the dull pinkish bill. "Gambell's" is a western form that has white in front of the eye, not black as in eastern birds.

The **white-throated sparrow** has a white throat, and most have a spot of yellow in front of the eye. It also seems to have little or no neck; the head sits squarely on the shoulders, while the white-crowned shows more neck.

Heads of both species can be striped in shades of brown instead of black and white. Brown stripes on a white-crowned sparrow are the mark of a young bird. On a white-throated, brown stripes are also worn by some adults. Very young birds of both species have brown streaks on their breasts.

84

very young
late summer

White-throated Sparrow

tan-striped
form

very young
late summer

young

White-crowned Sparrow

Gambell's
form

TREE SPARROW

FIELD SPARROW

CHIPPING SPARROW

The swamp sparrow resembles a chipping sparrow in winter. It is a shy wetland bird with a long rounded, not notched, tail and no dark eyeline.

The tree sparrow and the chipping sparrow are both regular backyard birds. Chipping sparrows like front lawns and unpaved driveways as well or better. Field sparrows are shy birds, more likely seen in the brush or briars of a park or nature center.

Not all plumages of these closely related, small, slim sparrows show a rusty cap or crown stripes, but most do. All three have fairly long, notched tails, and all flock in winter. (Tail shape is a good clue for identifying small brown sparrows.) The **tree sparrow** is a winter visitor with a prominent "stickpin" on its plain breast.

Best marks for the **field sparrow** are its bright pink bill and the white eye-ring. The eye-ring on the relatively plain face gives the bird a blank look.

Chipping sparrows have a bright rusty crown in summer, bordered by a white eyebrow and a black eyeline that extends all the way to the bill. They are summer visitors over much of the East, replacing the tree sparrows that migrate to the Arctic to nest. The face and crown are duller in winter, especially in first-winter birds. The black eyeline is not as bold in winter but still extends in front of the eye.

86

Tree Sparrow

very young
late summer

very young
late summer

Field Sparrow

Chipping Sparrow

very young
late summer

1st winter

summer

STREAKED SPARROWS

SONG SPARROW

SAVANNAH SPARROW

FOX SPARROW

The savannah sparrow has several color variations, including a very pale form known as the Ipswich sparrow that winters on coastal dunes in the Northeast.

Brown streaking on the breast is an important mark for song, savannah, and fox sparrows. Although clear-breasted sparrows show breast streaks when they are young, most streaks are lost soon after they leave the nest.

Not all birds with streaked breasts are sparrows, however. See the brown thrasher (p. 44), the female red-winged blackbird (p. 48), the young cowbird (p. 50), the pine siskin (p. 78), and the female finches (p. 80).

Song sparrows are common on the ground in backyards. The fox sparrow also visits backyards but is wary and reluctant to come out from cover. Like the brown thrasher (p. 44) and the eastern towhee (p. 74), it feeds in the ground litter under shrubs and brush. Savannah sparrows are seen in agricultural fields, grassy roadsides, and parks.

The center spot on the breast often used to identify **song sparrows** is not a conclusive mark; fox sparrows have it and so do many savannahs. The song sparrow's heavy black whisker mark and long rounded tail should also be noted. **Savannah sparrows** have a short notched tail and usually a lighter whisker. Many have a yellow spot in front of the eye. The **fox sparrow** is a large rusty red bird with especially bright color on the tail and rump.

88

Song Sparrow

young

Savannah Sparrow

Fox Sparrow

ooner or later all bird-watchers, even the most casual, wonder how many different species they have seen or how many have visited their backyards. Keeping a record is the only way to know. A list of species seen can become part of the pleasure of bird-watching.

Your backyard list can be put to scientific use by the Cornell Lab of Ornithology. Their Project FeederWatch, begun in 1987 as a joint US-Canadian project with Bird Studies Canada, compiles the counts of backyard birders. Participants receive a research kit and a quarterly newsletter of feeder-watch results for a low annual fee. For more information, call 1-800-843-2473 (1-519-586-3531 in Canada).

✓ Species		Date	Location
◯	RED-WINGED BLACKBIRD *Agelaius phoeniceus*[1]	48	....
◯	EASTERN BLUEBIRD *Sialia sialis*	58	....
◯	BOBWHITE Northern Bobwhite[2] *Colinus virginianus*	30	....
◯	INDIGO BUNTING *Passerina cyanea*	78	....
◯	CARDINAL Northern Cardinal *Cardinalis cardinalis*	74	....
◯	CATBIRD Gray Catbird *Dumetella carolinensis*	58	....

[1] Names in *italics* are the scientific names adopted by the American Ornithologists' Union.
[2] When the AOU English name differs from the common name used in this guide, the official AOU English name is given on the second line.

✓ Species	Date	Location

◯ BLACK-CAPPED **C**HICKADEE 70
Parus atricapillus

◯ CAROLINA **C**HICKADEE 70
Parus carolinensis

◯ BROWN-HEADED **C**OWBIRD 50
Molothrus ater

◯ BROWN **C**REEPER 38
Certhia americana

◯ AMERICAN **C**ROW 46
Corvus brachyrhynchos

◯ FISH **C**ROW 46
Corvus ossifragus

◯ MOURNING **D**OVE 32
Zenaida macroura

◯ ROCK **D**OVE 32
Columba livia

COMMON GROUND-DOVE
see **G**ROUND-DOVE

◯ HOUSE **F**INCH 80
Carpodacus mexicanus

◯ PURPLE **F**INCH 80
Carpodacus purpureus

◯ YELLOW-SHAFTED **F**LICKER 36
Northern Flicker
Colaptes auratus

◯ GREAT CRESTED **F**LYCATCHER 42
Myiarchus crinitus

◯ BLUE-GRAY **G**NATCATCHER 72
Polioptila caerulea

◯ AMERICAN **G**OLDFINCH 78
Carduelis tristis

◯ COMMON **G**RACKLE 46
Quiscalus quiscula

◯ EVENING **G**ROSBEAK 76
Coccothraustes vespertinus

✓ Species	Date	Location
○ ROSE-BREASTED **G**ROSBEAK 76 *Pheucticus ludovicianus*	....	....
○ COMMON **G**ROUND-DOVE 32 *Columbina passerina*	....	....
○ COOPER'S **H**AWK 24 *Accipiter cooperii*	....	....
○ RED-TAILED **H**AWK 22 *Buteo jamaicensis*	....	....
○ SHARP-SHINNED **H**AWK 24 *Accipiter striatus*	....	....
○ RUBY-THROATED **H**UMMINGBIRD 28 *Archilochus colubris*	....	....
○ BLUE **J**AY 48 *Cyanocitta cristata*	....	....
○ DARK-EYED **J**UNCO 82 *Junco hyemalis*	....	....
○ **K**ESTREL 22 American Kestrel *Falco sparverius*	....	....
○ EASTERN **K**INGBIRD 40 *Tyrannus tyrannus*	....	....
○ GOLDEN-CROWNED **K**INGLET 72 *Regulus satrapa*	....	....
○ RUBY-CROWNED **K**INGLET 72 *Regulus calendula*	....	....
○ PURPLE **M**ARTIN 26 *Progne subis*	....	....
○ EASTERN **M**EADOWLARK 54 *Sturnella magna*	....	....
○ **M**OCKINGBIRD 48 Northern Mockingbird *Mimus polyglottos*	....	....
○ COMMON **N**IGHTHAWK 18 *Chordeiles minor*	....	....

✓ Species	Date	Location

○ RED-BREASTED **N**UTHATCH 38
  Sitta canadensis

○ WHITE-BREASTED **N**UTHATCH 38
  Sitta carolinensis

○ BALTIMORE **O**RIOLE   52
  Icterus galbula

○ ORCHARD **O**RIOLE   52
  Icterus spurius

○ BARN **O**WL   18
  Tyto alba

  EASTERN SCREECH-OWL
  see **S**CREECH-OWL

○ RING-NECKED **P**HEASANT 30
  Phasianus colchicus

○ EASTERN **P**HOEBE   42
  Sayornis phoebe

  PIGEON
  see ROCK **D**OVE

○ AMERICAN **R**EDSTART   68
  Setophaga ruticilla

○ **R**OBIN   56
  American Robin
  Turdus migratorius

○ EASTERN **S**CREECH-OWL 18
  Otus asio

○ CHIPPING **S**PARROW   86
  Spizella passerina

○ FIELD **S**PARROW   86
  Spizella pusilla

○ FOX **S**PARROW   88
  Passerella iliaca

○ HOUSE **S**PARROW   82
  Passer domesticus

✓ Species		Date	Location
◯ SAVANNAH **S**PARROW *Passerculus sandwichensis*	88	....	....
◯ SONG **S**PARROW *Melospiza melodia*	88	....	....
◯ TREE **S**PARROW American Tree Sparrow *Spizella arborea*	86	....	....
◯ WHITE-CROWNED **S**PARROW *Zonotrichia leucophrys*	84	....	....
◯ WHITE-THROATED **S**PARROW *Zonotrichia albicollis*	84	....	....
◯ **S**TARLING European Starling *Stumus vulgaris*	50	....	....
◯ BARN **S**WALLOW *Hirundo rustica*	26	....	....
◯ TREE **S**WALLOW *Tachycineta bicolor*	26	....	....
◯ CHIMNEY **S**WIFT *Chaetura pelagica*	28	....	....
◯ SCARLET **T**ANAGER *Piranga olivacea*	54	....	....
◯ BROWN **T**HRASHER *Toxostoma rufum*	44	....	....
◯ WOOD **T**HRUSH *Hylocichla mustelina*	56	....	....
◯ TUFTED **T**ITMOUSE *Parus bicolor*	70	....	....
◯ EASTERN **T**OWHEE *Pipilo erythrophthalmus*	74	....	....
◯ BLUE-HEADED **V**IREO *Vireo solitarius*	60	....	....
◯ RED-EYED **V**IREO *Vireo olivaceus*	60	....	....

✓ Species	Date	Location

○ WARBLING VIREO 60
Vireo gilvus

○ BLACK VULTURE 20
Coragyps atratus

○ TURKEY VULTURE 20
Cathartes aura

○ BLACK-AND-WHITE WARBLER 68
Mniotilta varia

○ BLACK-THROATED GREEN WARBLER 64
Dendroica virens

○ CHESTNUT-SIDED WARBLER 62
Dendroica pensylvanica

○ MAGNOLIA WARBLER 64
Dendroica magnolia

○ MYRTLE WARBLER 62
Yellow-rumped Warbler
Dendroica coronata

○ YELLOW WARBLER 66
Dendroica petechia

○ CEDAR WAXWING 40
Bombycilla cedrorum

○ DOWNY WOODPECKER 34
Picoides pubescens

○ HAIRY WOODPECKER 34
Picoides villosus

○ RED-BELLIED WOODPECKER 36
Melanerpes carolinus

○ HOUSE WREN 44
Troglodytes aedon

○ WINTER WREN 44
Troglodytes troglodytes

○ COMMON YELLOWTHROAT 66
Geothlypis trichas

GRAB YOUR BINOCULARS AND THE CORNELL BIRD LIBRARY GUIDES

Sponsored by the Cornell Lab of Ornithology

THE WILDLIFE GARDENER'S GUIDE TO HUMMINGBIRDS AND SONGBIRDS FROM THE TROPICS

ISBN 0-06-273742-2 (paperback)

The definitive guide to identifying, attracting, and understanding the habits and habitats of hummingbirds and songbirds (such as orioles, grosbeaks, tanagers, thrushes and warblers) that migrate from the tropics to the U.S. and Canada each summer to nest. Also includes a section on natural history and basic identification.

THE BLUEBIRD MONITOR'S GUIDE TO BLUEBIRDS AND OTHER SMALL CAVITY-NESTERS

ISBN 0-06-273743-0 (paperback)

All the information necessary to attract small birds to a backyard nest box, including:

- Bird identification tips and descriptions
- Where to place nest boxes
- How to monitor the boxes without disturbing nesting
- How to protect the boxes from predators, parasites, and non-native species
- Sample nest box designs

THE FEEDERWATCHER'S GUIDE TO BIRD FEEDING

ISBN 0-06-273744-9 (paperback)

Based on the observations
and scientific documentation
of 15,000 bird-watchers, this
book details how to attract,
identify, and understand your
backyard feeder birds.
Topics include:

- How to attract winter birds
- Problems of pests and predators
- Species descriptions
- Identification problems
- Species count per region

DON'T FORGET YOUR FIELD GUIDE

From the American Bird Conservancy

ALL THE BIRDS OF NORTH AMERICA

ISBN 0-06-052770-6 (paperback)

A surer, faster, easier way to
identify birds. Everything you
need to know to enjoy bird
watching is at your fingertips.
Simply follow the unique keying
system based on the distinct
feeding strategies and
adaptations of each species.

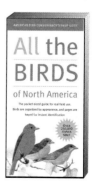

Available wherever books are sold,
or call 1-800-331-3761 to order.

 HarperResource

JACK GRIGGS, author of *All the Backyard Birds,* is an information designer and backyard bird-watcher who created the unique organization system used in this guide and in the American Bird Conservancy field guide, *All the Birds of North America.*

PAUL LEHMAN, ornithological editor of the American Bird Conservancy's compact guides, is the past editor of *Birding* magazine, the publication of the American Birding Association. He was a principal consultant on *All the Birds of North America* and on the *Audubon Society Master Guide to Birding.* His expertise in bird identification and distribution has made him a popular tour guide leader throughout North America.

SCOTT EDWARDS, who authored the foreword on attracting birds to your backyard, has been feeding birds and helping others enjoy this pastime for many years. He is a columnist for the New Jersey Audubon Society magazine and owner of a Wild Bird Center in Aston, Pennsylvania.

Want to Help Conserve Birds?
It's as Easy as ABC!

By becoming a member of American Bird Conservancy (ABC) you can help ensure work is being done to protect many of the species in this field guide. Join ABC today and you can read about the latest developments in bird conservation. You will receive four annual issues of *Bird Conservation* magazine and three issues of the newsletter *Bird Calls*. Together, these publications provide the most comprehensive overview of what's happening in all of bird conservation today as well as information on ways you can get involved.

Help make a difference to birds. Copy this page and mail to the address listed below.

☐ *Yes!* I want to become a member and receive *Bird Conservation* magazine. A check in the amount of $18 is enclosed.

☐ *Yes!* I want to become a member of ABC and receive *Bird Conservation* AND the newsletter *Bird Calls*. A check in the amount of $40 is enclosed.

Name: _____

Address: _____

_____

Return to: American Bird Conservancy, P.O. Box 249, The Plains, VA 20198 or call 1-800-BIRDMAG or email: abc@abcbirds.org.